THE GRAMMAR HANDBOOK

Part One
Elementary/Intermediate ESL

Nancy Clair
illustrations by Patrick R. Moran

Second, Revised Edition

Interplay ESL

Published by Pro Lingua Associates
15 Elm Street
Brattleboro, Vermont 05301
802-257-7779 800-366-4775

SAN 216-0579

At Pro Lingua,
our objective is to foster
an approach to language learning and teaching which
we call **Interplay**, the **inter**action of language
learners and teachers with their materials,
with the language and the culture, and
with each other in active, creative,
and productive **play**.

Copyright © 1984, 1990 by Nancy Clair

All rights reserved. No part of this publication may be represented or transmitted in any form or by any means, electronic, mechanical, photocopying, recording, or other, or stored in an information storage or retrieval system except for classroom use, without permission in writing from the publisher.

The cartoons by Jean Jacques Sempé are reprinted from *Women and Children First!* by Sempé, published by The Stephen Greene Press of Brattleboro, Vermont. They are used with the permission of the publisher, who reserves all rights to this material. The drawings on page 8 and 163 are Copyright © 1957, 1960, by PUNCH. The drawings on page 74 are Copyright © 1962 by Perpetua, Ltd.

ISBN 0-86647-042-5

This book was set in Century Oldstyle with the cover and titlepage in Tiffany by Stevens Graphics of Brattleboro, Vermont, and was printed and bound by Capital City Press of Montpelier, Vermont.

Designed by Arthur A Burrows.

Printed in the United States of America

Fourth printing, 1999
10,000 copies in print

Acknowledgements

As I sit back with my finished manuscript in front of me, I realize that there are many people who helped me directly and indirectly in writing this book.

First, I want to say thanks to all in the English Department at The Experiment in International Living in Brattleboro, Vermont. Thanks to Lisa Brodkey, Pam Helmick, Jackie Blencowe, Janie Duncan, Paul LeVasseur and Bobbi Williams. Thanks not only for your many teaching suggestions, but for your support too. And thanks also to Diane Larsen-Freeman of the Master of Arts in Teaching Program at the School for International Training for her advice, support and an advance copy of her invaluable book, *The Grammar Book*.

This book wouldn't have been possible if it weren't for my students in the International Students of English Program at The Experiment in International Living. Thanks to all of you for letting me try new techniques, experiment with old ones, and learn.

A special thanks goes to Ray Clark and Andy Burrows. Thanks Ray and Andy for helping me get started, having the confidence to let me go, and providing valuable suggestions along the way.

A major part of both editions of this book was written on the island of Puerto Rico and the port of Veracruz, Mexico. Sun, sand, and palm trees are conducive to writing grammar books. Thanks to Evelyn Montalvo, Milagros Rodriguez, in Puerto Rico, and to my Mexico MAT interns from the School for International Training in Veracruz.

In addition, I want to thank all of my colleagues who have shared their reactions and comments on the first edition. Many of their ideas and suggestions have gone into the second edition. Finally, thanks to Nick.

Nancy Clair
Veracruz 1990

Contents

Preface vi

Introduction vii

General 1
    1. Affirmative word order   1
    2. Negative word order   4
    3. Affirmative (Yes/No) questions   7
    4. Short answers   10
    5. Subject question words: *who, what, which, whose*   13
    6. Object question words: *whom, what, which, whose*   16
    7. Question words: *when, where, how, why*   19
    8. Contractions   22
    9. Tag questions   25
    10. Compound sentences   28

Nouns 31
    11. Regular plural nouns   31
    12. Irregular plural nouns   34
    13. Non-count nouns   37
    14. Possessive forms   40

Pronouns 43
    15. Subject pronouns   43
    16. Direct object pronouns   46
    17. Indirect object pronouns   49
    18. Possessive pronouns   52
    19. Possessive adjectives   55
    20. Expletive *it*   58
    21. Expletive *there is/are*   61

Verbs 64
    22. *To be* — Present tense   64
    23. *To be* — Past tense   67
    24. Simple present tense   70
    25. Simple present with stative verbs   73
    26. Present progressive tense   76
    27. Simple past tense   79
    28. Irregular past forms   82
    29. Future — *going to*   85

30. Future — *will*   88
31. Imperative   91
32. Imperative — *Let's*   94
33. Polite requests   97
34. Modals of ability — *can, be able to*   100
35. Modals of permission — *may, can*   103
36. *Have* and *have got*   106
37. Two-word verbs — separable   109

Adjectives   112
38. Definite article — *the*   112
39. Indefinite article — *a/an*   115
40. *Some/any*   118
41. Demonstratives — *this/that; these/those*   121
42. Numbers: cardinal and ordinal   124
43. Sequence of adjectives   127
44. Nationality   130
45. Comparative constructions   133
46. Superlative constructions   136
47. Quantity words   139

Adverbs   142
48. Adverbs of manner   142
49. Adverbs of frequency   145

Prepositions   148
50. Prepositions of time   148
51. Prepositions of place and position   151
52. Prepositions of direction   154

Appendix   157
Irregular verbs   157
Word groups   158

Essay on the Interplay Approach   161

Index of grammar and key words   165

Bibliography   166

Preface

The Grammar Handbook: Part One is the first book in the collection of language textbooks we have been publishing under the general title of *Interplay ESL*. Some teachers have used it as a student text for use in the classroom. Others have used it as a teacher resource and idea book complementing either our *Grammar Exercises: Part One* or other less grammar-focused materials such as *Side by Side* or our *Max in America*.

The first edition has been used in a great variety of programs: public school ESL classes from middle school on up, large adult refugee programs, small group tutorials, and EFL courses in several countries overseas. It has even been used in teacher training courses in which the teachers are asked to experiment with and evaluate the many techniques suggested. Over the last six years, we have gotten a lot of feedback, and our ideas have evolved. This revised edition is the result. There are more and better exercises using illustrations and a greater variety of the student-centered, communicative activities suggested for each lesson.

In the appendix starting on page 161, we have included a description of our *Interplay Approach* and of *Interplay ESL*.

For more information on how to use this *Grammar Handbook*, we urge you to study the introduction carefully.

Pro Lingua Associates
Arthur A. Burrows
Raymond C. Clark
Patrick R. Moran

Introduction

It is important that both the teacher and the students understand these general points.

1. **This book is designed for in-class use.** All the activities suggested in this book are based on classroom interplay, interactions between the teacher and students and among the students. Although the focus of this work is increasing mastery of English grammar, this is achieved through student-centered, communicative activities.

2. **This book stresses the importance of play.** Many of the activities involve creative work, real communication, and the playing of language games. Students will learn more, more easily, when the class is fun, when cooperation prevails over competition and stress, and when the approach to exploring the language is relaxed and enjoyable.

3. **There is a place for controlled exercises.** Although there are only a few drills and no fill-in-the-blanks exercises given in this book, many students benefit from this kind of work. The teacher can easily develop additional, more structured drills using the guidelines suggested in *Language Teaching Techniques*.

4. **This book may be supplemented with homework exercises.** It is designed to be used in programs in which students do not do grammar homework or to be used with *Grammar Exercises: Part One* or a comparable text.

5. **Students should write in their books.** This book is designed to be used as a workbook. If this is not possible, the students should be encouraged to keep their worksheets together in a notebook. Having the students' own words, phrases, sentences, paragraphs, stories, and notes — their creative efforts — together in one place and particularly in their own books results in a meaningful record of what happened in class and makes review more interesting and effective. Later on in their studies when they use this book as a reference grammar by checking back on a grammar point which they have studied, the lesson will come alive for them if their work is right in the book with the grammar explanation.

6. **This book covers the most basic English grammar.** However, it is not for absolute beginners. Most elementary level students have studied some grammar and can speak and read a little English. This book is for these "false" or "launched" beginners. It can also be used by more advanced, intermediate students who need to review the basics and to learn to use them accurately in speaking and writing. Because the activities are communicative and challenge the students to use all the English they know creatively, elementary and intermediate students will not find this book predictable, repetitive, and boring.

7. **You don't have to start on page one.** The 52 grammar points covered in this book are, of course, given in a sequence. For example, grammar relating to the use of verbs or prepositions, is grouped together. This sequence may be useful in doing a general review of the grammar. However, it is not necessary to follow it. The book is intended to be as flexible as possible. The teacher may want to put together his or her own sequenced grammar syllabus, starting, for example, with the imperative and following up with the present simple, the progressive, and so on. Or the teacher may use it interacting with the students. If they are having difficulty with irregular plural nouns or modals, the teacher can respond to their need by turning to those lessons in the book.

8. **The general format of each lesson is the same.**

    - *A concise explanation of the grammar* point with a paradigm and/or sample sentence of the type the teacher might put on the board. This is useful in making the initial presentation of the grammar. The presentation is not intended to be complete and detailed; it is a starting point for exploration.

    - *A writing exercise* in which the students write original sentences using their own vocabulary and subject matter following the pattern of sample sentences. This exercise focuses the students' attention on the structure in question. The sentences may be generated by the class working as a whole, in small groups or pairs, or by individuals working alone and then sharing some of their work.

    - *A selection of activities* providing an opportunity to practice the grammar point in an active, communicative context. These are given as suggestions for the teacher. It is not anticipated that all or only these activities will be used. The teacher should choose those which he or she feels the students need or which they have expressed an interest in — more advanced students may be motivated by choosing their own activities. Some of the choices are marked (LAB) to indicate that they are easily done in a language laboratory.

- *One of the activities in each lesson makes use of the illustration* or other graphic material given on the second page of the lesson. In some lessons, these illustrations may be supplemented by additional materials brought to class by the teacher or the students.

- *References.* The students are referred to the corresponding lesson in *Grammar Exercises: Part One* and in some cases to appropriate work in *Side by Side*. The references for the teacher are intended to give the teacher more information on teaching techniques and additional in-depth grammatical descriptions to supplement the concise descriptions in this book.

The approach to language teaching and learning upon which this book and its complement, *Grammar Exercises: Part One* are based is called *Interplay*. It is described in the appendix.

Affirmative word order 1

A sentence usually has three parts, in this order:

Subject	Verb	Complement
Winter	*is*	*cold*
Lisa	*plays*	*the viola.*

In the space below write sentences about your classmates.

Ligia is Mexican.
Guy speaks French.

1. _____
2. _____
3. _____
4. _____
5. _____
6. _____
7. _____
8. _____
9. _____
10. _____
11. _____
12. _____
13. _____
14. _____
15. _____
16. _____
17. _____
18. _____

1 Affirmative word order

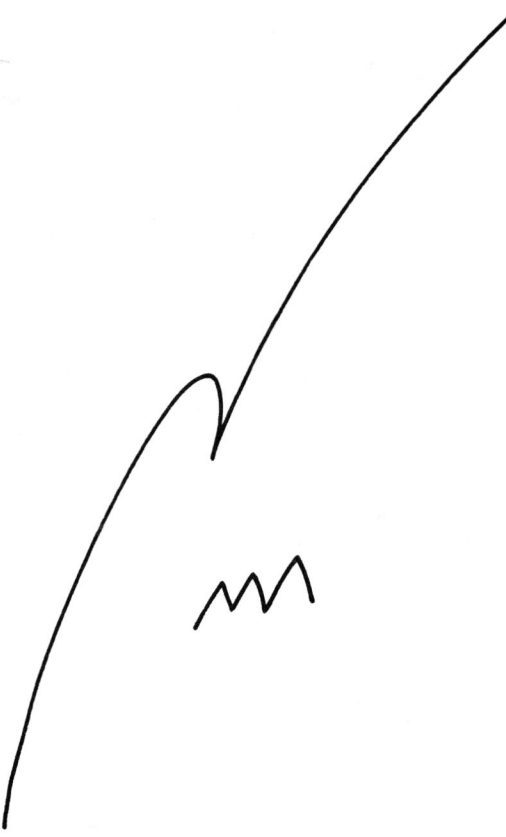

Finish the picture. Then, in the space below, write a story about your picture. Take special care with word order.

Affirmative word order 1

Activities

A. Picture Play
   1. Each student starts with a scribble and draws whatever it suggests to her or his imagination.
   2. She or he writes a story (or a few sentences) suggested by the picture.
   3. The students exchange their stories and check the word order. The teacher asks them to put any sentences they disagree on up on the board. The class solves the problem.
   4. Variation: It may be helpful if the teacher starts with a model—put a different scribble on the board, change it into a funny or poetic picture, either write a story complete with mistakes or ask the students to volunteer sentences, and then correct the story cooperatively as a class.

B. Word Play
   1. Choose one of the word groups in the Appendix on pages 158 to 160.
   2. The students create sentences or a dialogue using the words from the list.

C. Conversation
   1. The teacher shows the class a picture.
   2. The students talk about the picture. (Student utterances can be taped.)
   3. The teacher takes notes about word order mistakes. (Not necessary if taped)
   4. When all the students have contributed sentences, the teacher puts word order mistakes on the board. (Directly from the tape, if applicable)
   5. In pairs, the students correct the sentences.

D. Scrambled Sentences*
   1. Before class, the teacher writes sentences, putting each word in the sentence on an individual 3 x 5 card. The sentences could be about the class.
   2. Scramble the cards.
   3. In class, the students put the sentences back in order.

E. Oral Practice
   1. Write a noun on the board.
   2. Make different sentences using the word on the board, first in the subject, then in the complement.

References

For the Student
   Grammar Exercises, Part One, Burrows, pp. 1-4.

For the Teacher
   *1. *Index Card Games for ESL*, Clark, p. 31.
   2. *Modern English: A Practical Reference Guide*, Frank, p. 220.

2 Negative word order

> A sentence may be made negative in two ways:
>
> 1. **Not** follows the verb **to be**.
>
> | + | | | | − | | | |
> |---|---|---|---|---|---|---|---|
> | S | V | C | | S | V | N | C |
> | Nori | is | Japanese. | | Nori | is | **not** | Japanese. |
> | I | am | Venezuelan. | | I | am | **not** | Venezuelan. |
>
> 2. All other verbs are made negative by adding an auxiliary. **Not** follows the auxiliary.
>
> | + | | | | | − | | | | |
> |---|---|---|---|---|---|---|---|---|---|
> | S | A | V | C | | S | A | N | V | C |
> | Nino | | eats | meat. | | Nino | does | **not** | eat | meat. |
> | Nino | | ate | meat. | | Nino | did | **not** | eat | meat. |
> | Nino | will | eat | meat. | | Nino | will | **not** | eat | meat. |

Write a negative sentence in the space below. Write about yourself or your classmates.

Ligia is not Venezuelan.
Guy does not speak Italian.

1. _____
2. _____
3. _____
4. _____
5. _____
6. _____
7. _____
8. _____
9. _____
10. _____

Negative word order

2 Negative word order

Activities

A. Word Play
1. Put the following verbs on the board: *have, need, like* and *be*.
2. The students make negative sentences using the verbs.

B. Oral Practice
1. In pairs, Student A makes an affirmative statement. For example: *I like scuba diving.* Student B responds, *You're pulling my leg. You don't like scuba diving.*
2. Then Student B makes an affirmative statement. Student A responds in the negative.
3. After three minutes the students can switch partners and continue.
4. Variation: The teacher posts a variety of expressions appropriate to the age of the students and they choose and practice those which interest them. For example: *Get off it! You're kidding! Right! Get real!*

C. Crazy Ads
1. Use the illustration on page 5 or bring into class a short passage or paragraph from an advertisement.
2. The students rewrite the copy in the negative. To start the exercise, use an example from the ads (*Let's play tag!* > *Let's not play tag!*) or make up a line and have the students change it.

D. Conversation Game
1. Divide the blackboard in half with one side marked affirmative, the other negative.
2. Brainstorm affirmative expressions. For example: *I like, I love*, etc.
3. Brainstorm negative expressions. For example: *I don't like, I despise*, etc.
4. Student A chooses a topic and talks in the affirmative using the expressions you have brainstormed.
5. Student B, at any given moment, says, *change*.
6. Student A continues in the negative.
7. The change is repeated several times.

References

For the Student
> *Grammar Exercises, Part One*, Burrows, pp. 5-9.

For the Teacher
> *Modern English: A Practical Reference Guide*, Frank, pp. 87-88.

7 Affirmative (Yes/no) questions 3

Questions are formed in two basic ways:

1. The subject follows the verb **to be.**

+			?		
S	**V**	**C**	**V**	**S**	**C**
Urs	*is*	*Swiss.*	*Is*	*Urs*	*Swiss?*
Evelyn	*is*	*hungry.*	*Is*	*Evelyn*	*hungry?*

2. For all other verbs, the subject follows the auxiliary when there is already an auxiliary present.

+				?			
S	**A**	**V**	**C**	**A**	**S**	**V**	**C**
He	*will*	*go*	*home.*	*Will*	*he*	***go***	*home?*
She	*can*	*eat*	*meat.*	*Can*	*she*	***eat***	*meat?*

When there is no auxiliary present, the auxiliary **do** (**does, did**) is added. The subject follows **do** and the main verb is put in the simple form.

+			?			
S	**V**	**C**	**A**	**S**	**V**	**C**
Emie	*likes*	*ice cream.*	*Does*	*Emie*	*like*	*ice cream?*
Tareq	*needed*	*money.*	*Did*	*Tareq*	*need*	*money?*

Write questions in the space below.

Is Tuyen Vietnamese?
Does Rosalinda like the class?

1. _____
2. _____
3. _____
4. _____
5. _____
6. _____
7. _____
8. _____

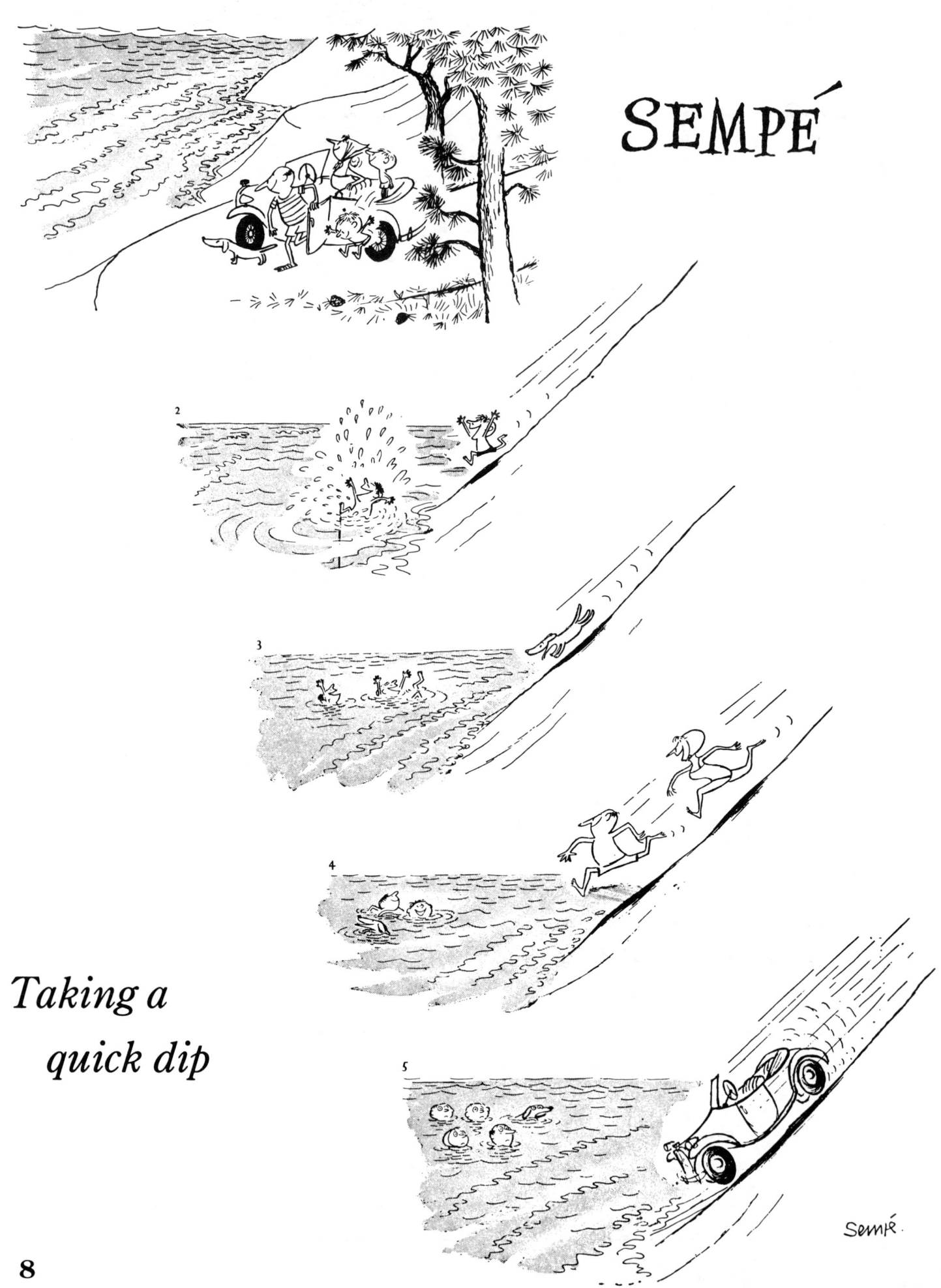

Affirmative (Yes/No) questions

Activities

A. Oral Practice
1. The students study "Taking a quick dip" by Sempé, or the teacher shows them another set of pictures which tells a story.
2. The students tell the story.
3. In pairs the students ask each other yes/no questions about the story for additional detail, expansion, and review.

B. Scrambled Sentences*
1. Each student writes one question about another student.
2. The teacher checks the questions.
3. The student puts each word on an individual 3 x 5 card.
4. Scramble the cards.
5. Exchange the scrambled questions and put them back in order.

C. Question Game
1. Place an object in a paper bag.
2. The students ask only yes/no questions until they guess what is in the bag.
3. The teacher takes notes or tapes student responses, and then writes the incorrect questions on a ditto or the blackboard.
4. The students make corrections.
5. A variation: Make one or two students responsible for bringing an object of their choice to class. This way the game can be played for several days, ensuring much student practice.

References

For the Student
1. *Side by Side, Book 1*, Molinsky, Bliss, pp. 24-31, 56, 60, 93-98.
2. *Grammar Exercises, Part One*, Burrows, pp. 10–12.

For the Teacher
*1. *Index Card Games*, p. 31.
2. *Story Squares: Fluency in English as a Second Language*, Knowles, Sasaki.
3. *The Grammar Book*, Celce-Murcia, Larsen-Freeman, pp. 107-121.
4. *Modern English: A Practical Reference Guide*, Frank, p. 88.

4 Short answers

We often answer affirmative (YES/NO) questions with short answers. A short answer has three parts:

1. **To be**
   Yes/No, the Subject, and the Verb (**to be**).

?			Short answer			
V	S	C	Y/N	S	V	N
Are	you	happy?	Yes,	I	am.	
			No,	I	am	not.
Is	Cuchy	tired?	Yes,	she	is.	
			No,	she	is	not.

2. All other verbs
   Yes/No, the Subject and the Auxiliary.

?				Short answer			
A	S	V	C	Y/N	S	A	N
Do	you	speak	French?	Yes,	I	do.	
				No,	I	do	not.
Can	Lisa	play	the viola?	Yes,	she	can	
				No,	she	can	not.

Answer the questions you wrote on page 7.

Is Tuyen Vietnamese? Yes, she is.
Does Rosalinda like the class? No, she does not.

1. _____
2. _____
3. _____
4. _____
5. _____
6. _____

Short answers 4

A. Solzhenitsyn

Martina Navratilova

Jane Fonda

Jesse Jackson

4 Short answers

Activities

A. True or False Game
   1. On the blackboard the teacher writes three sentences about him or herself — two true and one false.
   2. By asking questions, the students must guess which sentence is false.
   3. Students write three statements (two true and one false) about themselves.
   4. In groups, students ask each other questions to determine which statements are false.

B. Chain Drill*
   1. The teacher asks Student A: *Are you Mexican?*
   2. Student A answers: *Yes, I am* and asks Student B the same question.
   3. Student B answers. *No, I'm not. I'm Puerto Rican.*
   4. Student B asks Student C: *Are you Puerto Rican?* etc.

C. Conversation Game
   1. With the class, brainstorm questions you would ask if you had amnesia and wanted to know who you were. For example: *Am I male? Do I speak Spanish?*
   2. Have the students working in pairs ask and answer the questions they have brainstormed about the people pictured on page 11. One person takes the part of the person pictured.
   (Note: Steps 1 and 2 are preparation for the "famous people" game in steps 3, 4 and 5. Stronger students may not need them.)
   3. Write the names of famous people on index cards (one for each student).
   4. Tape the card on the back of each student. The students must not see who they are.
   5. The students circulate, asking each other questions like those in step 1 in order to discover who they are.

References

For the Student
   1. *Side by Side, Book 1,* Molinsky, Bliss, pp. 19-20, 24-30, 56-60.
   2. *Grammar Exercises, Part One,* Burrows, pp. 13–15.

For the Teacher
   *1. *The Grammar Book,* Celce-Murcia, Larsen-Freeman, p. 118.
   2. *Modern English: A Practical Reference Guide,* Frank, pp. 89-90.

Subject question words 5

Subject question words **Who, What, Which** or **Whose** can replace the subject of a sentence.

Who — refers to people
What — refers to things
Which and **whose** — refer to people or things

What, which and **whose** can be used alone or with a noun.

S/QW	V	C
Ray	needs	advice
Who	needs	advice?
Something	happened	yesterday.
What	happened	yesterday?
This	is	better.
Which	is	better?
Juan's paper	is	the best.
Whose	is	the best?

In the space below, write statements and questions about your country.

Washington was the first president of the U.S.
Who was the first president of the U.S.?
Washington is the capital of the U.S.
What is the capital of the U.S.?

1.
2.
3.
4.
5.
6.

5 Subject question words   14

What's the Question?*

CATEGORIES MONEY $	OUR CLASS	OUR COMMUNITY	WORLD GEOGRAPHY	FAMOUS PEOPLE
$5.00				
$10.00				
$15.00				
$20.00				

✿This game is similar to the popular T.V. game show **Jeopardy**.

Subject question words 5

Activities

A. Written/Oral Practice
1. The students write five sentences about their countries. Example: *Brasilia is the capital of Brazil.*
2. The students switch papers with each other.
3. The students write questions from the sentences.
4. In pairs, the students ask each other the questions.
5. The students make scrambled sentences of the questions and answers.*

B. What's the Question?
1. The teacher prepares answers to the categories on page 14. Other more relevant categories may be substituted.
2. Divide the class into teams. Team One chooses a category and a dollar amount.
3. The teacher reads the answer, and Team One provides the question. To be accepted, the question must be grammatically and informationally correct.
4. Encourage the students to make questions using subject question words.

C. Oral Practice**
1. Each student does something different: Student A: Combs her hair, Student B: sleeps; etc.
2. The teacher asks Student B: *Who is combing her hair?* Student B: *Tomoko is.*
3. The teacher asks Student B: *Whose comb is Tomoko using?* Student B: *Her comb.*
4. The students continue the activity by asking and answering questions.

References

For the Student

    Grammar Exercises, Part One, Burrows, pp. 16–19.

For the Teacher
  *1. *Index Card Games for ESL*, Clark, p. 31.
   2. *Modern English: A Practical Reference Guide*, Frank, pp. 92-93.
**3. *The Grammar Book*, Celce-Murcia, Larsen-Freeman, pp. 147-159.

6 Object question words 16

When **whom**, **what**, **which** or **whose** replace the object of the question, the word order is the same as a regular question.

O/QW	A	S	V	C(O)
	Did	*Koh*	*see*	*your doctor?*
Whom*	*did*	*Koh*	*see?*	
What	*did*	*Koh*	*see?*	
Which (doctor)	*did*	*Koh*	*see?*	
Whose (doctor)	*did*	*Koh*	*see?*	

*In conversation, **who** is often used instead of **whom**.

In the space below write pairs of statements and questions using **whom, what, which, whose**.

You have my dictionary.
Whose do you have?

1.
2.
3.
4.
5.
6.
7.
8.

Object question words 6

INTERVIEW				
student	*language*	*country*	*occupation*	*hobby*

?  ?

6 Object question words

Activities

A. Interview
1. Fill in the chart on the previous page by asking classmates the following questions:
   a. *What is your name?*
   b. *What language do you speak in your country?*
   c. *Which country do you come from?*
   d. *What do you do in your country?*
   e. *Which hobby do you like?*
2. Fill in another chart by finding students from another class, school personnel, or anyone else and asking them the same interview questions.

B. Written Practice
1. The teacher divides the class into groups.
2. The teacher gives each group a large piece of brown paper with a sentence on it. Example: *Kiko dances with his friends every Saturday night.*
3. Put question words under the sentence: **whom, what, which, whose.**
4. The students write questions.
5. Switch papers; the students correct each other's papers.

C. Oral Practice
1. The teacher puts on the blackboard an information chart like the one on the previous page.
2. List several students on the chart.
3. The students take turns asking questions about the individuals listed. For example: *What country does Shu come from? Which language does Romy speak? What is Maria's hobby?*
4. One of the students fills in the chart on the board.

References

For the Student
   Grammar Exercises, Part One, Burrows, pp. 21-24.

For the Teacher
   The Grammar Book, Celce-Murcia, Larsen-Freeman, pp. 147-159.

Question words 7

With **when, where, how** and **why,** we use the word order of regular questions.
Remember: with the verb **to be**, the subject follows the verb.

?	V	S	C
	Is	*Mishiko*	*unhappy?*
When	*is*	*Mishiko*	*unhappy?*

All other verbs require an auxiliary with the original verb in the simple form.

?	A	S	V	C
	Did	*Mishiko*	*go*	*home?*
Where	*did*	*Mishiko*	*go?*	
When	*will*	*Mishiko*	*go?*	
How	*can*	*Mishiko*	*go?*	

In the space below write questions using **when, where, how, why**.

When is your birthday?
Where do you live?

1.
2.
3.
4.
5.
6.
7.
8.
9.
10.
11.
12.

7   Question words

Find someone who

1. can juggle
2. was born in September.
3. is a twin.
4. speaks more than two languages.
5. is a baseball fan.
6. is a vegetarian.
7. likes rock music.
8. is from Czechoslovakia.
9. has more than 3 brothers and 3 sisters.
10. has traveled 7 continents.

Activities

A. Find someone who . . .
1. The students fill in page 20 by asking classmates, friends, school personnel, or family members the questions suggested by the list. For example: *Can you juggle?*
2. They may wish to share interesting information they learn while doing the assignment. (This is a good activity for getting to know one another, an icebreaker.)

B. Story Squares*
1. The teacher introduces the characters pointing to each one. *This is Cassie. This is Kathy.*
2. The teacher gives the class the basic information: *Cassie takes a bus in the morning, etc.*
3. Practice the information with the class by pointing to the character and the square.
4. Practice the question words **when, where, who** by pointing to a question word and then a box. Example: *When does Kathy take a bus?*
5. After the students have practiced orally, they write three questions for each question word.
6. Variation: the students can add more to the story: *Where does Kathy take the bus? Why?* etc.

C. Conversation/Written Practice—A Dramatic Event
1. Ask someone who is not part of the class, to interrupt your class unexpectedly. Example: Another teacher can run into your class wildly saying she has just quit. Then she runs out.
2. As a class, re-tell the scene.
3. In groups, the students write questions about what happened.

References

For the Student
1. *Side by Side, Book I,* Molinsky, Bliss, pp. 2, 3, 8, 14, 15, 32, 34.
2. *Grammar Exercises, Part One,* Burrows, pp. 25-28.

For the Teacher
*1. *Story Squares,* Knowles, Sasaki, pp. 9-13.
2. *The Grammar Book,* Celce-Murcia, Larsen-Freeman, pp. 147-159.
3. *Modern English: A Practical Reference Guide,* Frank, pp. 91-93.

8 Contractions

We often use the following **negative** contractions in spoken English:

do not — don't   are not — aren't
does not — doesn't   is not — isn't
did not — didn't   was not — wasn't
will not — won't   were not — weren't

We often use the following **affirmative** contractions:

I am — I'm   I will — I'll
you are — you're   you will — you'll
he is — he's   he will — he'll
she is — she's   she will — she'll
it is — it's   it will — it'll
we are — we're   we will — we'll
they are — they're   they will — they'll

In the space below write pairs of sentences using a contraction in the second sentence.

Asuka did not understand Paul.
Asuka didn't understand Paul.

1.
2.
3.
4.
5.
6.

Contractions

TIC TAC TOE

did not	you will	I am
will not	they are	we are
do not	she is	it will

TIC TAC TOE

Make your own game and play with your classmates

8 Contractions

Activities

A. Written Practice
1. The teacher gives the students a short paragraph.
2. The students rewrite the paragraph making all possible changes to contractions.

B. Tic Tac Toe
1. On the blackboard, make a Tic Tac Toe grid.
2. Put uncontracted words in the blocks.
3. Divide the class into Team X and Team O.
4. A student chooses a square and makes the contraction.
5. To make the game more challenging, make a correct sentence with the contraction.
6. They can use the top grid on page 23 and then make up their own games. Students can practice in small groups or pairs.

C. Matched Pairs*
1. Write 15 full forms on 15 different index cards.
2. Write 15 matching contractions on 15 additional cards.
3. Shuffle all 30 cards and turn them face down. Number the backs from 1 to 30.
4. The students match the full form with the contraction.
5. Variation: students can use the contractions in a complete sentence.

References

For the Student

Grammar Exercises, Part One, Burrows, pp. 29–32.

For the Teacher
*1. *Index Card Games,* Clark, p. 3.
2. *Modern English: A Practical Reference Guide,* Frank, pp. 87, 107–108.

Tag questions

There are two kinds of **tag questions**; they both have two parts:

1. Affirmative Tag Questions (+, − ?)
   We use an affirmative statement (+) followed by a negative tag question (−).

Statement		**Usual response (agreement)**
+	**−**	**+**
Naki is a Turk,	*isn't he?*	*Yes, he is.*
You live in Russia,	*don't you?*	*Yes, I do.*

2. Negative Tag Questions (−, + ?)
   We use a negative statement (−) followed by an affirmative tag question (+).

−	**+**	**−**
You don't eat meat,	*do you?*	*No, I don't.*
She isn't Salvadoran,	*is she?*	*No, she isn't.*

Tag questions are generally used when we want to confirm information that we already know. Notice that the response to a tag question is usually agreement. However, it is possible to respond with disagreement.

+	**−**	**−**
It's usually warm in Greenland,	*isn't it?*	*No, it isn't.*

In the space below, write tag questions. Practice both the affirmative and the negative.

You speak Cantonese, don't you?
He doesn't like rock and roll, does he?

1.
2.
3.
4.
5.
6.
7.
8.

9

Tag questions 26

Fill in blanks with appropriate statements or tags. Then make up your own. Switch papers and have a classmate make any necessary corrections.

1. This snowman has six buttons, _____?

2. My heart isn't broken, _____?

3. James caught _____ fish, _____ he?

4. There are four lions, _____?
   That goat should run, _____?

5. _____, don't you?

6. _____, isn't he?

7. You'll go to the party, _____?

8. _____, does he?

9. She studied for the exam, _____?

10. _____, _____?

11. _____, _____?

12. _____, _____?

Activities

A. Matched Pairs*
   1. Write 15 statements on 15 different index cards.
   2. Write 15 matching tag endings.
   3. Shuffle the cards and turn them face down.
   4. The students try to match the tag with the statement.

B. Written Practice
   1. Divide the class into groups.
   2. Have each group work together to complete page 26, or give each group a large piece of brown paper with statements and tag endings similar to those on page 26.
   3. The students complete the questions.
   4. The groups exchange papers and correct each other's work.

C. Eavesdrop**
   1. The teacher asks the students to listen to a conversation in the cafeteria, on the bus, etc.
   2. The students listen and jot down the tag questions they hear.
   3. In class, the students share what they have heard.

References

For the Student
   1. *Side by Side, Book II,* Molinsky, Bliss pp. 174-177.
   2. *Grammar Exercises, Part One*, Burrows, pp. 33-36.

For the Teacher
   *1. *Index Card Games,* Clark, p. 3.
   2. *Modern English: A Practical Reference Guide*, Frank, pp. 89-90.
   **3. *Experiential Language Teaching Techniques*, Jerald, Clark, pp. 11-15.

10 Compound sentences

English sentences can be connected by **and, but, or**:

And: one thought is added to another.
*This flag is Puerto Rican, **and** that flag is American.*

But: one thought is contrasted to another.
*Ricardo went to the movies, **but** I didn't go.*

Or: one thought is the alternative to the other.
*You can have soup, **or** you can have salad.*

A comma is used between the two thoughts.

In the space below write sentences with **and, but,** and **or**.

I like beer, but Yoshi likes wine.
We can go to the dance, or we can stay here.

1.
2.
3.
4.
5.
6.
7.
8.
9.
10.
11.
12.
13.
14.
15.
16.

Compound sentences

10 Compound sentences

Activities

A. Using the Environment*
   1. The students search for several signs, posters, or ads that can be rewritten to form compound sentences. They can use school announcments and signs in store windows as well as newspaper and magazine ads.
   2. The students copy the original words on page 29 and then rewrite them. For example: *Mole's Eye Cafe—Our Mexican Specialties are hot, but our live music is even hotter!*
   3. The students share the meaning and contexts of the sentences they find.
   4. An additional twist: the teacher explains that compound sentences are rarely used in signs or ads and challenges the students to find some.

B. Oral Practice**
   1. Ask one student two things she likes to do.
   2. Student A: *I like to swim. I like to dance.*
   3. Ask another student to connect the two sentences.
   4. Ask one student one thing she likes and one thing she doesn't like to do.
   5. Student B: *I like to ski. I don't like to fall.*
   6. Ask another student to connect the two sentences.
   7. Finally, break the class into small groups. Give each group a picture and have them write five compound sentences.

C. Role Play***
   1. In groups of two or three, the students write dialogues about a restaurant scene, trying to use compound sentences.
   2. Use the vocabulary list on page 160 to help.
   3. Perform the dialogues.

References

For the Student
   1. *Side by Side, Book 1,* Molinsky, Bliss, pp. 24, 25, 132, 133.
   2. *Grammar Exercises, Part One*, Burrows, pp. 37-39.

For the Teacher
   *1. *Experiential Language Teaching Techniques,* Jerald, Clark, pp. 21-25.
   **2. *The Grammar Book,* Celce-Murcia, Larsen-Freeman, pp. 295-307.
   ***2. *Language Teaching Techniques,* Clark, pp. 55-58.
   3. *Modern English: A Practical Reference Guide,* Frank, pp. 223-228.

Regular plural nouns

Nouns are usually made plural by adding an **s**
- viola — viola**s**
- squirrel — squirrel**s**

With nouns ending in **s, x, z, ch, sh,** we add **es.**
- bus — bus**es**
- class — class**es**

With nouns ending in **y** preceded by a consonant, we change the **y** to **i** and add **es.**
- lady — lad**ies**
- company — compan**ies**

With nouns ending in **o** preceded by a consonant, we add **es.**
- echo — echo**es**
- tomato — tomato**es**

In the space below, write singular and plural nouns.

stereo   stereos
culture   cultures

1.
2.
3.
4.
5.
6.
7.
8.
9.
10.

11 Regular plural nouns

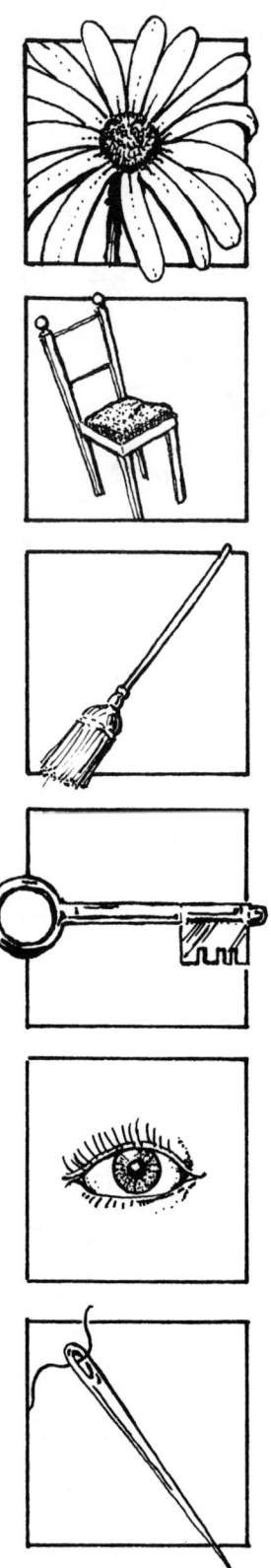

Regular plural nouns 11

Activities

A. Word Play
1. The teacher gives the class a picture with several items in it.
2. The students study the picture for one minute; then they list singular and plural forms of all the items they can remember.

B. Spelling Practice (LAB)
1. The teacher says a noun in the singular.
2. The students write the plural

C. Matched Pairs*
1. On index cards write 15 nouns which have regular plurals. Choose 5 nouns each which take the endings **-s**, **-es**, and **-ies**. For example: *clock, zero, baby*.
2. On 15 other cards write the matching endings. For example: *-s, -es, -ies*.
3. Shuffle the cards and turn them face down.
4. The students in turn choose a card, turn it over, and then try to find a card with the matching ending. If they guess correctly, they keep the pair of cards and make another choice. If incorrectly, they turn the cards back facedown and the next student chooses.
5. When all the pairs have been picked up, the student with the most pairs wins.
6. Variation: Divide the class into teams and ask each team to make up a set of cards. Check their work. The teams then swap sets of cards.
7. Variation: When a student finds a match, he must put the plural in a sentence pronouncing it correctly.

D. Word Play
1. The teacher asks the students one at a time to contribute a noun which has a regular plural and then lists the singular form on a sheet of brown paper or the blackboard. The list should have about ten nouns.
2. The students then pair up to write sentences using as many of the nouns as possible in each sentence. The nouns must be used in the plural form.
3. The teams are asked to volunteer to share their work with the class.

References

For the Student
1. *Side by Side, Book I,* Molinsky, Bliss, pp. 41-43.
2. *Grammar Exercises, Part One,* Burrows, pp. 40-43.

For the Teacher
*1. *Index Card Games for ESL,* Clark, p. 3.
2. *Modern English: A Practical Reference Guide,* Frank, p. 13.

12 Irregular plural nouns 34

> Some nouns have irregular plural forms.
>
> | Singular | Plural |
> |----------|--------|
> | woman | women |
> | man | men |
> | child | children |

In the space below write as many irregular plural nouns as you can. Use your environment to give you clues.

foot   feet
life   lives

1.
2.
3.
4.
5.
6.
7.
8.
9.
10.
11.
12.
13.
14.
15.
16.
17.
18.
19.
20.
21.
22.
23.
24.
25.
26.
27.
28.
29.
30.
31.
32.
33.
34.
35.
36.
37.
38.
39.
40.
41.

Irregular plural nouns

Across
1. Small children often lose this but they get a new one.
2. If you have brothers and sisters you are one of many _____.
3. Sharks have many of these.
4. These fall in autumn.
5. This bird is native to North America.
6. These can be found in the Maine woods.
7. The central parts of atoms.

Down
6. Few people like this animal in their house.
8. These are found in water.
9. If you have no brothers and sisters you are an only _____.
10. What can you use to cut something? (plural)
11. These animals are very strong.
12. This part of the body is attached to your ankles.

12   Irregular plural nouns

Activities

A. Written/Oral Practice*
   1. The teacher supplies the students with a list of irregular plural nouns.
   2. In pairs, the students construct dialogues, using the nouns.
   3. The students act out their dialogues.

B. Tic Tac Toe (see p. 23)
   1. On the blackboard make a grid.
   2. Put singular nouns in the blocks.
   3. Divide the class into Team X and Team O.
   4. The students choose the square and spell the irregular plural.

C. Crossword Puzzle
   1. The students fill in the crossword puzzle working in groups, in pairs, or individually.
   2. Correct the answers as a class.

D. Picture Sort Pairwork**
   1. The teacher collects pictures of single objects which have regular and irregular plurals and puts them in a paper bag.
   2. The students pull the pictures out one at a time and sort them into two piles, saying the plurals out loud as they work.
   3. Variation: the students working in two groups write skits using the items as props. Then they perform their skits for the other group.

References

For the Student
   Grammar Exercises, Part One, Burrows, pp. 44-47.

For the Teacher
   *1. *Language Teaching Techniques,* Clark, pp. 51-54.
   *2. *The ESL Miscellany,* Clark, Moran, Burrows, Grammar List 2 — Irregular Plurals.
   3. *Modern English: A Practical Reference Guide,* Frank, p. 13.
   **4. *Lexicarry: An Illustrated Vocabulary Builder for Second Languages*, Moran.

Non-count nouns   13

> Non-count nouns do not have a plural form. There are two kinds:
>
> 1. **Mass nouns** — Matter that is not easily counted.
>   - coffee
>   - sugar
>   - gold
>   - oxygen
>
> 2. **Abstract nouns** — Qualities, fields of study, sports.
>   - beauty
>   - chemistry
>   - philosophy
>   - soccer

In the space below, write as many non-count nouns as you can.

air, beer, cake, coffee
age, energy, life, truth

1.
2.
3.
4.
5.
6.
7.
8.
9.
10.
11.
12.
13.
14.
15.
16.
17.

13 Non-count nouns 38

Non-count nouns 13

Activities

A. Picture Sort Pairwork*
   1. The students look at the pictures on page 38 and identify both count and non-count nouns. Example: *cars, traffic*
   2. The teacher collects pictures of count and non-count objects* and puts them in a paper bag.
   3. The students take them out one at a time and sort them into count and non-count piles, making a sentence with the nouns.

B. Oral Practice
   1. Divide the blackboard into two halves: count and non-count.
   2. Ask the students to think about their hometowns.
   3. The teacher and the students put nouns on the board according to count/non-count. Example: traffic, pollution, restaurants, etc.
   4. In pairs, the students describe their hometowns to each other.
   5. Each student tells the rest of the class about his or her partner's hometown.

C. Written Practice

   Using the above activity as a basis, the students write descriptions or sentences about their hometowns.

D. Conversation
   1. The students collect some non-count nouns. Those on the preceding page may be used. Here are some others: *luggage, information, corn, bread, thunder, lightning.*
   2. Find out how to make the nouns countable. If possible, the students go out of class to ask native speakers.

E. Listening Practice (LAB)
   1. The teacher selects either a list of nouns** or a short passage and reads it.
   2. The students listen for the nouns and list the count/non-count nouns in two columns.

References

For the Student
   1. *Side by Side, Book I*, Molinsky, Bliss, pp. 112-115, 118-121.
   2. *The ESL Miscellany,* Clark, Moran, Burrows, Grammar List 8 — Non-count Nouns.
   3. *Grammar Exercises, Part One*, Burrows, pp. 48–50.

For the Teacher
   *1. *Lexicarry: An Illustrated Vocabulary Builder for Second Languages*, Moran.
   2. *Modern English: A Practical Reference Guide,* Frank, pp. 7, 126, 136-137.
   **3. *The ESL Miscellany,* Clark, Moran, Burrows, Topics Lists 1-53.

14 Possessive forms

To show possession:

1. Add **'s** to nouns not ending in **s**.
   Singular nouns — *The boy's book is on the desk.*
   Irregular plural nouns — *The children's toys are on the floor.*

2. Add **'** to nouns ending in **s**.
   Plural nouns — *The boys' books are on the desk.*
   Singular nouns *Grandma Moses' paintings are in Bennington, Vermont.*

3. For nouns referring to things, places or concepts, we often use **of** to indicate association, origin or source.
   *the legs **of** the table*
   *the center **of** Brattleboro*
   *the philosophy **of** science*

In the space below write sentences with possessives.

Katie's friends are nice.
The teachers' cars are in the lot.

14 Possessive forms

14 Possessive forms

Activities

A. Oral Practice*
   1. Collect pictures of people and items and make flash cards with them.
   2. Give the people names.
   3. Hold up a flash card and use the following pattern.
      Teacher: *What's this?* Student: *It's a knife.*
      Teacher: *Who's this?* Student: *It's Carmen.*
      Teacher: *Whose knife is this?* Student: *It's Carmen's.*
   4. The students can ask each other questions.

B. Written Practice*
   1. Supply the class with a paragraph containing blank lines and two noun phrases in parentheses. Example: *Last night I went to a party. It was _____ (my aunt/anniversary).*
   2. The students fill in the blanks.

C. Whose is whose?
   1. Using the characters and objects on page 41, the students write a story. They use as many possessives as they can.
   2. The students can just write sentences instead of a story.
   3. They exchange stories, and their partner suggests corrections.
   4. Variation: The teacher collects stories and writes one incorrect sentence from each story on a ditto.
   5. In pairs, the students correct the errors.

D. Conversation
   1. Each student briefly describes some of his/her favorite possessions.
   2. As they talk, the teacher draws symbols on the board to represent the possession.
   3. When all have finished, engage in a question-answer practice focused on the symbols on the board, e.g. *Whose guitar is this? It's Jorge's guitar.*

References

For the Student
   Grammar Exercises, Part One, Burrows, pp. 51–55.

For the Teacher
   *1. *The Grammar Book,* Celce-Murcia, Larsen-Freeman, pp. 124-128, 131-132.
   2. *Modern English: A Practical Reference Guide,* Frank, pp. 12, 15.

Subject pronouns

Pronouns are words that replace nouns. The subject pronouns are:

Singular	Plural
I	we
you	you
he, she, it	they

The subject pronoun replaces the subject of the sentence.

S	V	C
Pilar	*is*	*superstitious.*
She	*is*	*superstitious.*
The river	*is*	*wide.*
It	*is*	*wide.*

In the space below, write sentences using subject pronouns.

We are studying pronouns.
They danced all night.

1.
2.
3.
4.
5.
6.
7.
8.
9.
10.
11.
12.
13.
14.

15 Subject pronouns

Activities

A. Oral Practice
1. The teacher gives each student an assortment of colored rods.
2. Teacher: *Janie, please give a yellow rod to Oscar. Juan, what did Janie do?*
3. Student: *She gave a yellow rod to Oscar.*
4. Follow-up variation: the students can give the commands using objects in the classroom instead of rods.

B. Conversation
1. Show a map of the downtown area of your city or use the map of Smalltown on page 92.
2. Introduce the vocabulary.
3. In pairs, the students take turns imagining themselves doing some activity at a location on the map. The other student tries to find out what the first student is doing.

C. Oral/Written Practice
1. Use the pictures of people in various occupations on page 44 or find pictures in magazines.
2. Hold up the pictures and ask the students: *What is she?*
   Student: *She is a carpenter.*
3. The students write a sentence for each picture. The teacher asks: *What is she?*
4. Variation: The students mime occupations. The teacher asks: *What is she?*

References

For the Student
1. *Side by Side, Book I,* Molinsky, Bliss, pp. 5-9.
2. *Grammar Exercises, Part One,* Burrows, pp. 56-59.

For the Teacher
*1. *The Grammar Book,* Celce-Murcia, Larsen-Freeman, pp. 122-124, 131.
2. *Modern English: A Practical Reference Guide,* Frank, pp. 20-21.

16 Direct object pronouns

The object pronouns are:

Singular	Plural
me	us
you	you
him, her, it	them

Object pronouns are used as direct or indirect objects,* or as objects of prepositions.

S	V	IO	DO	O/P
Pam	understands		**him.**	
They	gave	**us**	a refrigerator.	
I	lived			near **them.**

*See pp. 49-51.

In the space below write sentences with direct object pronouns.

Bob saw them yesterday.
Hope is going to see us tomorrow.

1.
2.
3.
4.
5.
6.
7.
8.
9.
10.
11.
12.
13.
14.

Direct object pronouns 16

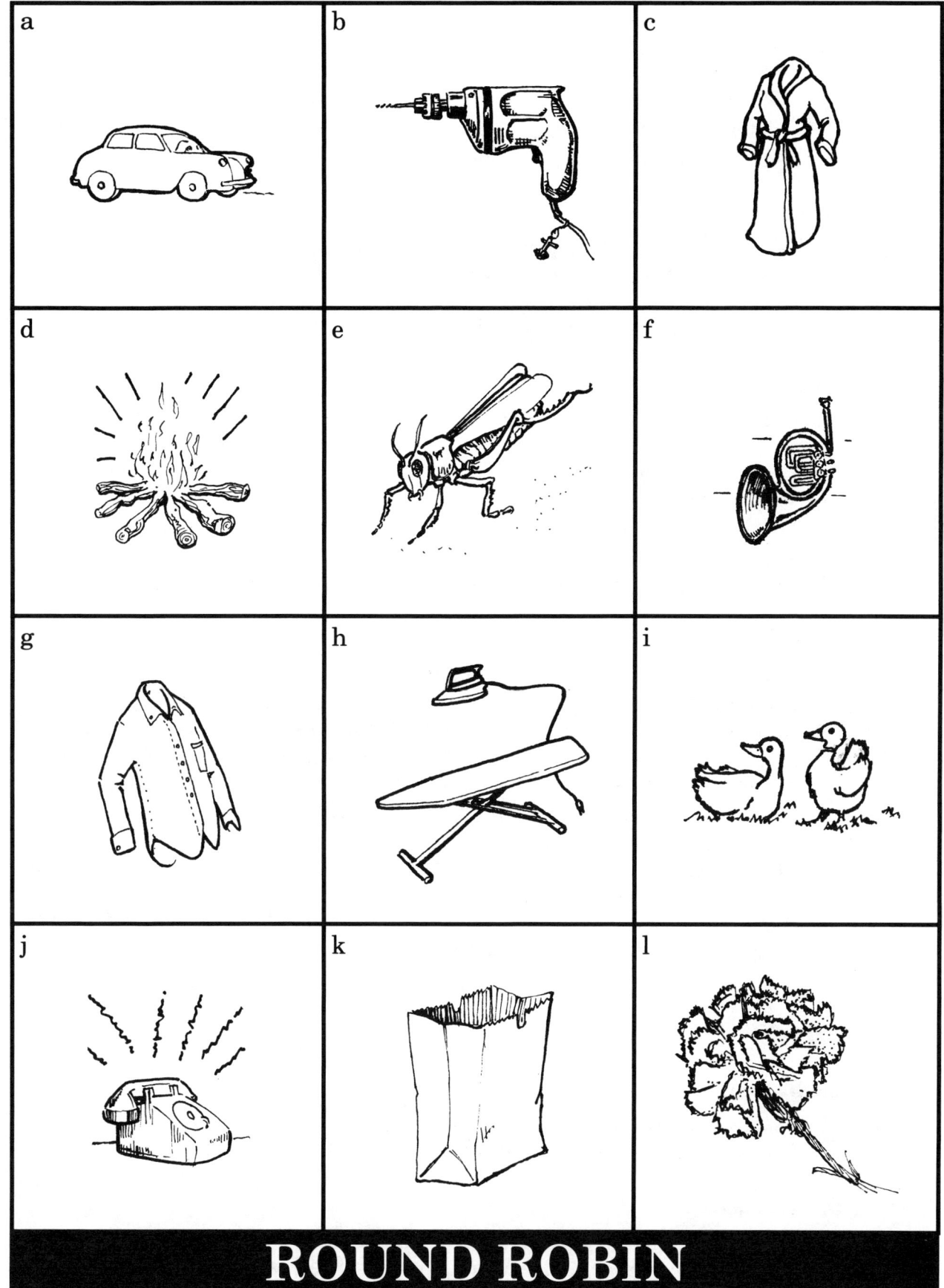

ROUND ROBIN

16 Direct object pronouns

Activities

A. Oral Practice (LAB)*
   1. The teacher gives sentences without object pronouns. Teacher: *I saw Shu.*
   2. The students substitute the object pronoun. Students: *I saw him.*

B. Oral Practice
   1. Give each student an assortment of colored rods.
   2. Teacher: *Take a blue rod and give it to Hope. What did you do?*
   3. Student: *I gave it to Hope.*
   4. Vary the practice with it and them.

C. Action Chain*
   1. Teacher: _____, *look at* _____. *What are you doing?*
   2. Student: *I'm looking at him.*
   3. Teacher: *Touch him.*
   4. Student: (Touches him)
   5. Teacher: *What did you do?*
   6. Student: *I touched him.*
   7. Some additional verbs might be: tickle, hit, punch, pinch, kick.

D. Round Robin
   1. The students identify the vocabulary pictured on page 47.
   2. Each student takes a piece of paper and writes a sentence at the top using any one of the words pictured. For example: *Ali drove my car on Monday.*
   3. The teacher can suggest that the students tell a story on each sheet of paper.
   4. Each paper is passed on to the next student who rewrites the sentence using an object pronoun (for example: *Ali drove it on Monday.*) and then writes another sentence using another word from page 47.
   5. The teacher may ask the students to take the pictures in order or let them choose words which interest them.
   6. When the story gets back to the original student, he or she corrects the grammar and then posts it for the class to see.

References

For the Student
   1. *Side by Side, Book 1,* Molinsky, Bliss, pp. 62-65.
   2. *Grammar Exercises, Part One,* Burrows, pp. 60–64.

For the Teacher
   *1. *Language Teaching Techniques,* Clark, pp. 105-108.
   2. *The Grammar Book,* Celce-Murcia, Larsen-Freeman, pp. 122, 124, 131.
   3. *Modern English: A Practical Reference Guide,* Frank, pp. 20-21.

Indirect object pronouns

The indirect object pronoun is the person to whom something is sent, told, given, etc. When the indirect object follows the direct object we use **to** or **for**.

S	**V**	**DO**	**IO**
He	gave	the money	**to me.**
She	baked	a cake	**for them.**

When the direct object follows the indirect object we do not use **to** or **for**.

S	**V**	**IO**	**DO**
He	gave	**me**	the money.
She	baked	**them**	a cake.

When both objects are pronouns the direct object must precede the indirect object.

S	**V**	**DO**	**IO**
She	gave	it	**to me.**

In the space below write three sentences with indirect object pronouns.

Jamie told the news to us last night.
Jamie told us the news last night.
Jamie told it to us.

1.
2.
3.
4.
5.
6.
7.
8.
9.

17

Indirect object pronouns

My Christmas List

Indirect object pronouns 17

Activities

A. Scrambled Sentences*
   1. Write sentences with indirect object pronouns. Put each word on an individual 3x5 card. You can use student-generated sentences.
   2. Scramble the cards.
   3. Put the sentences back in order.

B. Oral Practice
   1. The teacher gives each student an assortment of colored rods.
   2. Teacher: *Take a blue rod and give it to Hope. What did you do?*
   3. Student: *I gave it to her.*
   4. After the pattern is established the students can give commands.

C. Written Practice
   1. In pairs, two students mime a sequence of actions to the rest of the class. The teacher can give each pair a list of actions, such as: see, speak, shake (hands), say (goodbye).
   2. The observers write what they saw using direct and indirect pronoun objects.

D. Holiday Helper
   1. Each student makes up a holiday gift list for six or more people, including at least one couple ("my parents") and one favorite pet ("Rex, my dog"). It can be a list for Christmas (see page 50) or any other culturally appropriate holiday.
   2. Each "person" on the list should get one or more presents. Somebody should get more than one.
   3. In groups of three, each student explains his or her gifts. (The teacher may indicate the tense to be used.) For example: *I'm going to give my brother a Chrysler convertible.* Or, *I gave . . .*
   4. The other students take turns asking questions like: *Are you sure you're going to give him a Chrysler convertible?* or *Did you really give it to your brother?* The Holiday helper replies using both direct and indirect object pronouns, *Yes, I gave it to him.*
   5. For some classes, the teacher may want to put model sentences on the blackboard.

References

For the Student
   1. *Side by Side, Book I,* Molinsky, Bliss, pp. 108-109, 190-191.
   2. *Grammar Exercises, Part One*, Burrows, pp. 65–69.

For the Teacher
   *1. *Index Card Games For ESL*, Clark, p. 31.
   2. *Modern English: A Practical Reference Guide*, Frank, pp. 20, 21, 28.

18 Possessive pronouns

The possessive pronouns are:

Singular	Plural
mine	ours
yours	yours
his, hers, its	theirs

Possessive pronouns can be used alone as a subject, an object, or a complement.

Subject: *Mine is here.*
Object: *I gave mine to Ali.*
Complement: *That one is mine.*

In the space below write sentences with possesive pronouns, following the pattern of the sample.

Jackie has a new Toyota.
Hers is new.
I saw hers yesterday.
The new Toyota is hers.

1.

2.

3.

Possessive pronouns 18

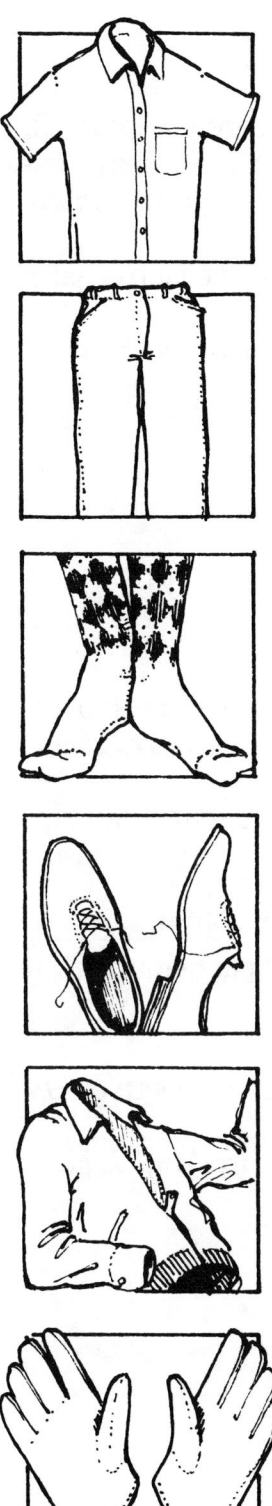

18 Possessive pronouns

Activities

A. Written Practice
1. Each student writes four sentences about the clothing pictured on page 53. They use possessive pronouns as subjects, objects, and complements following this pattern: *My gloves are brown. Hers are black. She left hers on the train. These are mine.*
2. Pairs of students exchange their sentences and read and correct each other's work.
3. To make the exercise shorter, the teacher may give the students a choice of two to five items of clothing.

B. Guessing Game*
1. Each student puts a small object under an overturned box.
2. The students should not see each other's objects.
3. Lift the box and guess whose object is whose. Example: *Marcia, is yours blue?*

C. Circle Practice
1. A student describes something he or she is wearing and then describes something similar belonging to another student. Student A: *My pants are green. Hers are denim.*
2. Student B does the same thing and then repeats the first student's description: Student B: *My sweater is blue. His is yellow. Her pants are green. Hers are denim.*
3. Student C continues, creating his sentence and then repeating all the others.
4. The activity continues until all students in the circle have participated.

D. Oral Practice (LAB)
1. The teacher gives the students a sentence with a possessive adjective: *My book is blue.*
2. The students change the sentence using a possessive pronoun: *Mine is blue.*

References

For the Student
1. *Side by Side, Book I,* Molinsky, Bliss, p. 134.
2. *Grammar Exercises, Part One*, Burrows, pp. 70–72.

For the Teacher
*1. *Communication Starters and Other Activities for the ESL Classroom,* Winn-Bell Olsen, p. 30.
2. *The Grammar Book,* Celce-Murcia, Larsen-Freeman, pp. 124, 131.

Possessive adjectives

Possessive adjectives show possession. They are:

Singular	Plural
my	our
your	your
his, her, its	their

Possessive adjectives modify the subject, object or complement. They cannot be used alone like other pronouns.

My tape is broken.
Is this your calculator?
Classroom 37 is our classroom.

In the space below, write sentences with possessive adjectives.

Alejandro has my coffee cup.
Your camera is broken.

1.
2.
3.
4.
5.
6.
7.
8.
9.
10.
11.
12.
13.
14.
15.

A Wedding Day to Remember

NOTTINGHAM, England (UPI) — Hayley and Ray Prescott deserve a long and happy married life after their dramatic wedding day.

"The day began badly," said Ray, "when my brother, aunt, and nephew cracked up my car." They were taken to the hospital. His car was a total wreck.

At the church no one could find the wedding ring. Ray's father offered to let Ray borrow his, but Hayley wanted her own. The best man and his wife had to go back to their apartment to get it.

After the ceremony everyone drove off to the reception, except for the bride, bridegroom, three bridesmaids, and the bride's mother.

"Our car didn't arrive," Hayley explained, "because Ray's cousin who was driving it had gone to the hospital. She was visiting her mother and her brother who were hurt in the accident." The minister did not have his car but offered to drive them in his wife's. He found it was out of gas.

After they finally got to their reception hall by taxi, the bride and groom found all their guests waiting outside. The cousin who went to the hospital had the key to the hall in her purse.

Finally, the hall was opened. Their photographer lined up the wedding party for the official wedding picture, and, of course, he had forgotten his film.

"At least my cake was a success," Hayley's mother reported." My daughter asked for it, you see. Chocolate peppermint is our family's favorite."

Possessive adjectives 19

Activities

A. Reading for Grammar — A Wedding Day
   1. The students read the newspaper article on page 56 and underline the possessive adjectives. They exchange papers and check each other's work.
   2. Alternatively, one student reads the story aloud. When the other students hear a possessive adjective they tap their desks with a pencil and then underline the word if the class agrees it is an adjective.

B. Written Practice
   1. The teacher dictates a short paragraph with a number of possessive pronouns.
   2. The students change the possessive pronouns to possessive adjectives.
   3. The teacher reads the paragraph again, writing it on a piece of large paper (or board) as she talks. The students correct their paragraphs.

C. Conversation
   1. Bring in a favorite photograph.
   2. In pairs, explain who is in the photograph, the relationship of the people, etc.

D. Oral Practice
   1. Each person puts a small object in a large paper bag. Then everybody draws one out.
   2. Each person asks one question. Example: *Saulo, is this your watch?*
   3. The objective is to identify the owner of each object using possessive adjectives. Try to accomplish it in one round of questions.

References

For the Student
   1. *Side by Side, Book I*, Molinsky, Bliss, pp. 18-21.
   2. *Grammar Exercises, Part One*, Burrows, pp. 73-76.

For the Teacher
   The Grammar Book, Celce-Murcia, Larsen-Freeman, pp. 124-131.

20 Expletive IT

> The impersonal subject **it** is used in expressions of weather, time, distance and identification.
>
>   Weather — ***It** is cold in Vermont.*
>   Time — ***It** is 5:30.*
>   Distance — ***It** is 100 miles from Mayaguez to San Juan.*
>   Identification — *Who is **it**? **It** is Nancy.*
>
> **It** is also used in the following constructions:
>
>   **It** + be + adjective, infinitive
>   ***It** is difficult to eat with chopsticks.*
>
>   **It** + be + adjective
>   ***It** is dark in here.*
>
> In speech, expletive **it** is almost always contracted to **it's**. It's often written in the contracted form.

In the space below write sentences using **it**.

It is very stuffy in this room.
It's a long way to Tipperary.

1. _____
2. _____
3. _____
4. _____
5. _____
6. _____
7. _____
8. _____
9. _____
10. _____
11. _____
12. _____
13. _____

NATIONAL WEATHER SERVICE FORECAST to 7 PM EST APRIL 20, 1942

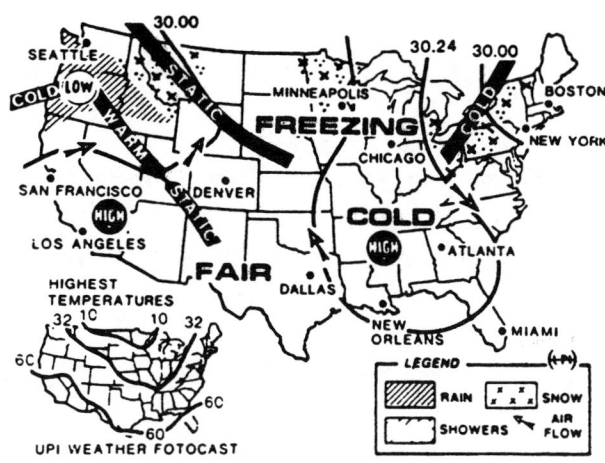

NATIONAL WEATHER FORECAST to 7 PM EST DECEMBER 16, 2010

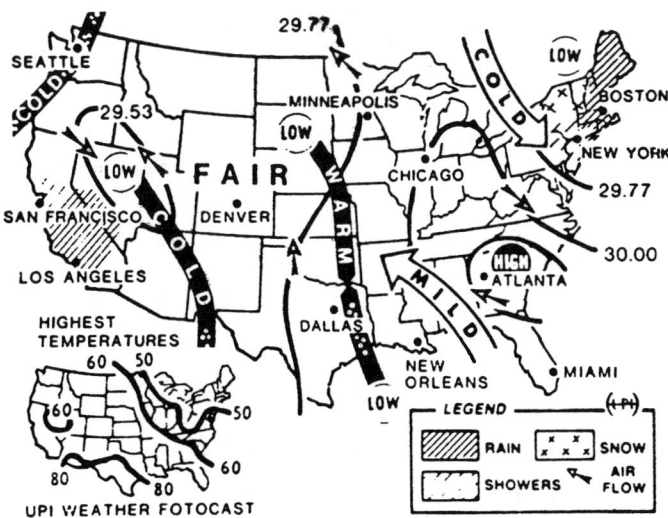

20 Expletive IT

Activities

A. Oral Practice
1. In pairs, the students ask each other about the weather in the capital cities of their countries.
2. Practice the following questions: *Is it sunny? Is it rainy?* etc.
3. Variations: use the weather maps on page 59 and have the students ask and answer questions about the cities shown. If they are able to do so, the students can use the past and future tenses appropriate to the dates on the maps.

B. Oral Practice
1. The teacher supplies each student with a map showing distances between a number of cities.
2. Teacher: *How far is it from Philadelphia to New York?* Student: *It is 95 miles.*
3. The students work in pairs with each other.
4. Variation: work with a city map, introduce new vocabulary, e.g., block, square, boulevard, etc.

C. Written Practice
1. Introduce weather vocabulary.*
2. Each person writes one paragraph about the climate in his or her city.
3. The students read their paragraphs aloud as classmates listen specifically for weather vocabulary. Then post the descriptions.

D. Conversation
1. The teacher asks the students to write down something that is difficult to do; easy to do; dangerous to do; fun to do; etc.
2. Compare and discuss the answers.

References

For the Student
  Grammar Exercises, Part One, Burrows, pp. 77–80.

For the Teacher
1. *The Grammar Book,* Celce-Murcia, Larsen-Freeman, pp. 280-294.
2. *Modern English: A Practical Reference Guide,* Frank, pp. 36-37.
*3. *The ESL Miscellany,* Clark, Moran, Burrows, Topics List 11 — Weather and Climate.

Expletive *THERE IS/ARE*

> **There is** is used with singular nouns.
>
> > *There is a star in the sky.*
> > *There is a child in the park.*
>
> **There are** is used with plural nouns.
>
> > *There are stars in the sky.*
> > *There are children in the park.*

In the space below, write sentences with **there is, there are**.

There are eight people in my family.
There's a hole in my pocket.

1.
2.
3.
4.
5.
6.
7.
8.
9.
10.
11.
12.
13.
14.
15.
16.
17.
18.

21 Expletive THERE IS/ARE

Activities

A. Interview

1. Brainstorm questions that you would ask if you were going to interview someone about their hometown.
2. The students ask each other about their hometowns, practicing questions with **there is** and **there are**.
3. The students can then interview other people — school personnel, friends, family members, etc.

B. Written Practice

1. To follow up the interviews in A., above, each person writes a page on *"My Hometown,"* leaving the name of the town or city and the writer off.
2. Post the compositions for all to see.
3. Try to guess the town and the author.

C. Oral Practice

1. Show the class a detailed picture of the inside of a house, or one specific room.* You can use the picture on page 62.
2. Go over any new vocabulary.
3. The students ask each other questions about what is in the picture, using **is there** and **are there**.

D. Skit: "There's a Fly in my Soup."**

1. Read the entire skit for comprehension and go over the vocabulary.
2. Assign two or more students to each role.
3. Act out the skit.

References

For the Student

1. *Side by Side, Book I*, Molinsky, Bliss, pp. 37-40.
2. *Grammar Exercises, Part One*, Burrows, pp. 81-87.

For the Teacher

*1. *Lexicarry, A Vocabulary Builder for Second Languages*, Moran, pp. 110-121.
2. *The Grammar Book,* Celce-Murcia, Larsen-Freeman, pp. 280-294.
3. *Modern English: A Practical Reference Guide*, Frank, pp. 37-39.
**4. *Skits in English As a Second Language*, Hines, pp. 1-3.

22 TO BE—present

The present tense of **to be** is:

Singular	*Plural*
I **am**	we **are**
you **are**	you **are**
he, she, it **is**	they **are**

*He **is** shy.*
*They **are** tall.*

In the space below, write sentences with the verb **to be**.

We are surprised.
She is flabbergasted.

1.
2.
3.
4.
5.
6.
7.
8.
9.
10.
11.
12.
13.
14.
15.
16.
17.
18.

65   *To BE*—present   **22**

name: _____
age: _____
residence: _____
profession: _____

name: _____
age: _____
residence: _____
profession: _____

name: _____
age: _____
residence: _____
profession: _____

name: _____
age: _____
residence: _____
profession: _____

name: _____
age: _____
residence: _____
profession: _____

name: _____
age: _____
residence: _____
profession: _____

name: _____
age: _____
residence: _____
profession: _____

name: _____
age: _____
residence: _____
profession: _____

name: Clark Kent
age: 75
residence: Metropolis
profession: SuperHero

name: _____
age: _____
residence: _____
profession: _____

22 To BE—present

Activities

A. Oral Practice*

1. As a class, construct a map of a city, including stores, offices, etc., or use the map of Smalltown on page 92.
2. Go over the new vocabulary.
3. Carry out a chain drill. The teacher starts. Teacher: *Where are you?*
4. Student A: *I'm in the post office. Where is Toshi?* Student B: *He's at the bank. Where's Mundeke?*, etc.

B. Characters in Search of an Author*

1. Each student chooses a character from those on page 65.
2. Variation: each student chooses a character from a collection of photos or pictures collected by the teacher from newspapers or magazines.
3. The students write down information about their characters in the space provided. They should be encouraged to add creative details.
4. Each student shows his or her picture to the class and takes about one minute to introduce him or herself.
5. The other students ask a few questions.
6. Tape record each student. Write a transcript on the board and have the students make corrections.
7. After a couple of students have introduced their characters, one of the others recapitulates what they have said.

C. Written Practice

1. Each student writes 5 to 10 sentences about him or herself, using **am**, e.g., *I am five-foot-two.* Do not put their names on the paper.
2. Shuffle and exchange papers.
3. Read the papers aloud, using **is**. Guess who it is written about.
4. Listen for opportunities to use **we** and **they**, e.g., *Heloisa, we are both five-foot-two.*

References

For the Student

1. *Side by Side, Book I*, Molinsky, Bliss, pp. 1-9, 24-25.
2. *Grammar Exercises, Part One*, Burrows, pp. 88–90.

For the Teacher

* *Language Teaching Techniques,* Clark, pp. 47-50.

TO BE—past

The past tense of **to be** is:

Singular	Plural
I **was**	we **were**
you **were**	you **were**
he, she, it **was**	they **were**

*I **was** thin.*
*We **were** quiet.*

In the space below, write sentences with the verb **to be** in the past tense.

It was rainy yesterday.
We were in Boston on Monday.

1.
2.
3.
4.
5.
6.
7.
8.
9.
10.
11.
12.
13.
14.
15.
16.
17.
18.

PERSONAL CHARACTERISTICS

Personality Traits	Physical Traits
shy	*tall*
quiet	*short*

To BE—past

Activities

A. Oral Practice

1. As a class, construct a map of a city, including offices, stores, etc., or use the map of Smalltown on page 92. Go over new vocabulary.
2. Each students writes down where they were yesterday and the day before.
3. Teacher: *Where were you yesterday?* Student A: *I was at the bakery.*
Teacher: *Where was (Student A) yesterday?* Student B: *She was at the bakery.*
Teacher: *(Student B), ask (Student C) where he was the day before yesterday.*
4. Once the question and answer pattern is established, the teacher allows the students to generate their own questions.

B. Written Practice

1. Brainstorm selected personality and physical characteristics.* See page 68.
2. The students write sentences describing themselves as a child.
3. The teacher collects the sentences and corrects them.
4. The teacher gives the papers back randomly and has the students copy the sentences on large pieces of brown paper.
5. Hang the papers up. The students must guess whose description is whose.

C. Who's Who?**

1. The students bring to class either photographs of themselves as children or magazine or newspaper pictures which look like them as children. Some students will probably bring in improbable pictures which adds to the fun.
2. The teacher collects the pictures without letting the other students see them and mounts the pictures on cardboard with the student's name on the back. The pictures are then divided into two piles and team lists made up.
3. At the next class, the students are assigned to the teams and given their own pictures. One member of the team holds up each picture in turn.
4. The other team tries to guess who's who. They have ten yes-or-no past tense questions. Example: *Javier, were you chubbier when you were young?*
5. The team with the most correct identifications wins.

References

For the Student

1. *Side by Side, Book I*, Molinsky, Bliss, pp. 100-104.
2. *Grammar Exercises, Part One*, Burrows, pp. 91-94.

For the Teacher

*1. *The ESL Miscellany,* Clark, Moran, Burrows, Topics List 9 — Human Qualities & Stages.
**2. *Index Card Games for ESL*, Clark, pp. 63-74.

24 Simple present

We form the simple present tense as follows:

Singular	**Plural**
I sleep	we sleep
you sleep	you sleep
he, she, it sleep**s**	they sleep

We add **es** to the 3rd person singular if:

1. a verb ends in **o**. *I go. She goes.*
2. a verb ends in **sh, ch, s, x,** or **z**. *I teach. She teaches.*
3. a verb ends in **y** preceded by a consonant. We change the **y** to **i**. *I study. She studies.*

We use the simple present tense to express:

1. Everyday actions. *He smokes after every meal.*
2. General truths. *The earth revolves around the sun.*
3. Stative (non-action) truths. (see p. 73) *I need a dime.*

In the space below, write sentences using the simple present tense.

We live in Philadelphia.
Bruno fixes cars.

1.
2.
3.
4.
5.
6.
7.
8.
9.
10.

A Typical Day in _____

Time	Activity

24 Simple present

Activities

A. Written Practice

Fill in the chart on the preceding page. Then write a short paragraph about a typical day in your country.

B. Oral Practice
1. On the board have a daily activity chart starting at *6:30 a.m.—get up* and ending *12 p.m.—go to sleep.*
2. Include different activities for each half-hour.
3. Go over the vocabulary.
4. Ask questions about the chart. Teacher: *What does Majid do at 6:30 a.m.?* Student: *He gets up.*
5. In pairs, the students can ask each other questions.

C. Oral/Written Practice
1. In pairs, the students interview each other about their daily habits in their native country.
2. The students write paragraphs about each other's daily activities.
3. Adverbs of frequency can be introduced at the beginning of the lesson.
4. Variation: students can interview school personnel, community members, friends, etc. They can work in pairs.*

D. Chart Pattern Practice** (LAB)
1. Refer to the chart on p. 161, in the appendix.
2. The teacher gives a cue. Teacher: *Six-thirty. Peter.*
3. The student responds: *Peter gets up at six-thirty.*

References

For the Student
1. *Side by Side, Book I,* Molinsky, Bliss, pp. 52-65.
2. *Grammar Exercises, Part One,* Burrows, pp. 95-98.

For the Teacher
1. *The Grammar Book,* Celce-Murcia, Larsen-Freeman, pp. 62, 74.
2. *Modern English: A Practical Reference Guide,* Frank, pp. 68-70.
*3. *Experiential Language Teaching Techniques,* Jerald, Clark, pp. 69-73.
**4. *Language Teaching Techniques,* Clark, pp. 73-76.

Simple present—stative

Stative verbs (non-action) are usually used in the simple present tense rather than the present progressive. They are:

1. Verbs of perception: **see, hear, feel, taste, smell.**
   *Pierre **feels** homesick.*

2. Verbs of emotion or mental state: **love, hate, know, believe,** etc.
   *Orawan **knows** the answer.*

3. Verbs of measurement: **weigh, measure, equal,** etc.
   *It **weighs** 10 kilos.*

4. Other non-action verbs: **have, need, want, owe,** etc.

In the space below, write sentences with stative verbs.

Sergio hates lab.
Abdul needs help.

1. _____
2. _____
3. _____
4. _____
5. _____
6. _____
7. _____
8. _____
9. _____
10. _____
11. _____
12. _____
13. _____

1.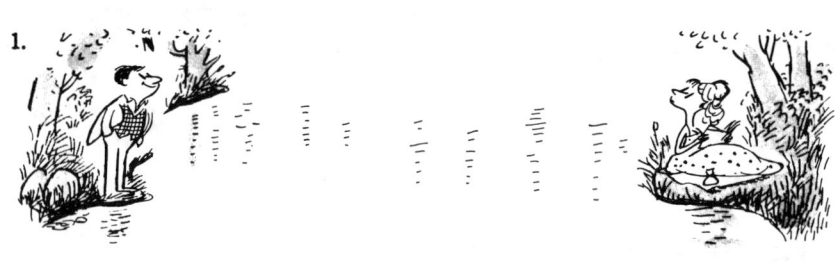

2.

3.

4.

5.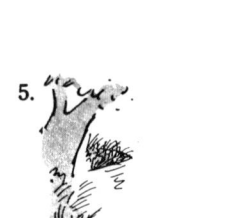

6.

7.

SEMPÉ

"The Rocky Road of Love"

8.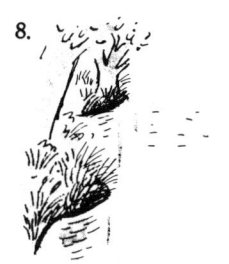

Simple present—stative

Activities

A. Oral/Written Practice — The Rocky Road
   1. The teacher shows the class a provocative picture. The cartoon on page 74 can be used.
   2. The class makes a list of emotion or mental state verbs on the board.
   3. Go over the verbs for meaning.
   4. The students write sentences about the picture using the verbs.
   5. Each student shares one sentence with the class.
   6. Variation: Working in pairs, more advanced students prepare a narrative to fit "The Rock Road of Love" and then record it. The class then listens to the tape, making a list of the stative verbs used. The pair which uses the most correctly is given a prize.

B. Conversation
   1. The teacher gives the students a questionnaire about their likes, dislikes or preferences on a selected topic. Food is a good topic.
   2. Discuss each question as a class.
   3. The teacher notes student errors, focusing on the verbs.
   4. The teacher puts the notes on a ditto.
   5. The students correct the errors.

C. Chain Drill
   1. Student A says: *My name is _____ and I like spaghetti.*
   2. Student B: *His name is _____ and he likes spaghetti. My name is _____ and I like motorcycles.*
   3. Continue around the circle until everybody has participated.

References

For the Student
   1. *Side by Side, Book I*, Molinsky, Bliss, pp. 52-65.
   2. *The ESL Miscellany,* Clark, Moran, Burrows, Grammar List 7 — Stative Verbs and Topics List 23 — Emotions.
   3. *Grammar Exercises, Part One*, Burrows, pp. 99-104.

For the Teacher
   1. *The Grammar Book,* Celce-Murcia, Larsen-Freeman, pp. 71-72.
   2. *Modern English: A Practical Reference Guide*, Frank, pp. 68-70.

26 Present progressive

We form the present progressive by using the verb **to be** and the present participle (**-ing** form) of the main verb.

Singular
I **am** sleep**ing**.
You **are** sleep**ing**.
He, She, It **is** sleep**ing**

Plural
We **are** sleep**ing**.
You **are** sleep**ing**.
They **are** sleep**ing**.

We use the present progressive to:

1. express an action in the present:
   Emmy is skiing now.
   It is raining.

2. express an action in the future:
   She is leaving tomorrow.
   I am calling home on Monday.

Notice the formation of questions and negative sentences.

Am I sleeping?
I am not sleeping.

In the space below, write about what is happening now.

I am reading this sentence now.

1. _____
2. _____
3. _____
4. _____
5. _____
6. _____
7. _____
8. _____
9. _____
10. _____

Present progressive 26

6:30

wake up

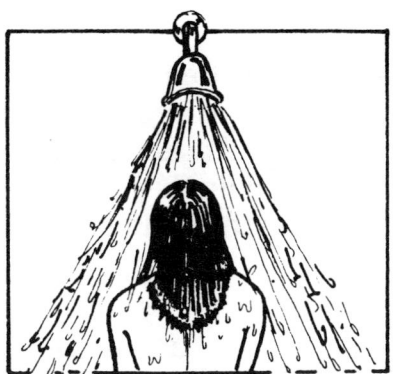
take a shower

get dressed

eat breakfast

leave home

study

leave school

watch TV

go to bed

26 Present progressive

Activities

A. Activity Charades
   1. The teacher writes an activity on a 3x5 card — at least one for each student. Example: Brush your teeth; write a letter; etc.
   2. Each student gets a card and acts out what is on his or her card.
   3. The other students guess what he or she is doing.
   4. Variation: Divide the class into teams. Limit the number of guesses.

B. Written Practice
   1. To contrast the simple present and present progressive, the teacher shows the class a large picture.
   2. Put a number of verbs on individual 3x5 cards. Include stative verbs.
   3. Divide the class in small groups and give each group a stack of verbs.
   4. The groups sort the verbs — simple present and present progressive.
   5. Each student writes sentences about the picture, using the verbs.

C. Chart Pattern Practice* (LAB)
   1. Use the chart on page 77.
   2. Teacher: *It's 6:30; what is Joan doing?* Student: *She is waking up.*
      Teacher: *What does Joan do every day at 6:30?* Students: *She wakes up.*
      Teacher: *What is she doing in the next picture? What does she do every day after she wakes up?*
   3. In pairs the students ask each other questions.

D. Postcards
   1. Write a class postcard to someone the class knows. Draw the postcard on a large piece of brown paper. Have one student write on the brown paper and, once the class has corrected any mistakes, have another write the postcard. Leave the brown paper posted as a model.
   2. The students write real postcards and send them to someone of their choice.
   3. Encourage them to use all the verb forms they have studied.

References

For the Student
   1. *Side by Side, Book I*, Molinsky, Bliss, pp. 11-16, 67-71.
   2. *Grammar Exercises, Part One*, Burrows, pp. 105–107.

For the Teacher
   1. *The Grammar Book*, Celce-Murcia, Larsen-Freeman, pp. 63, 74-77.
   2. *Modern English: A Practical Reference Guide*, Frank, pp. 70-72.
   *3. *Language Teaching Techniques*, Clark, pp. 73-76.

Simple past 27

We form the past tense by adding **-ed** to regular verbs.

Singular
I play**ed**
you play**ed**
he, she, it play**ed**

Plural
we play**ed**
you play**ed**
they play**ed**

We <u>use</u> the past tense to express a completed action in the past.

We played chess yesterday.

Notice the formation of questions and negative sentences.

***Did** you play?*
*You **did not** play.*

In the space below, write sentences in the simple past.

Rolf smoked a cigar last night.
Ali cooked dinner for us.

1.
2.
3.
4.
5.
6.
7.
8.
9.
10.
11.
12.
13.

27 Simple past

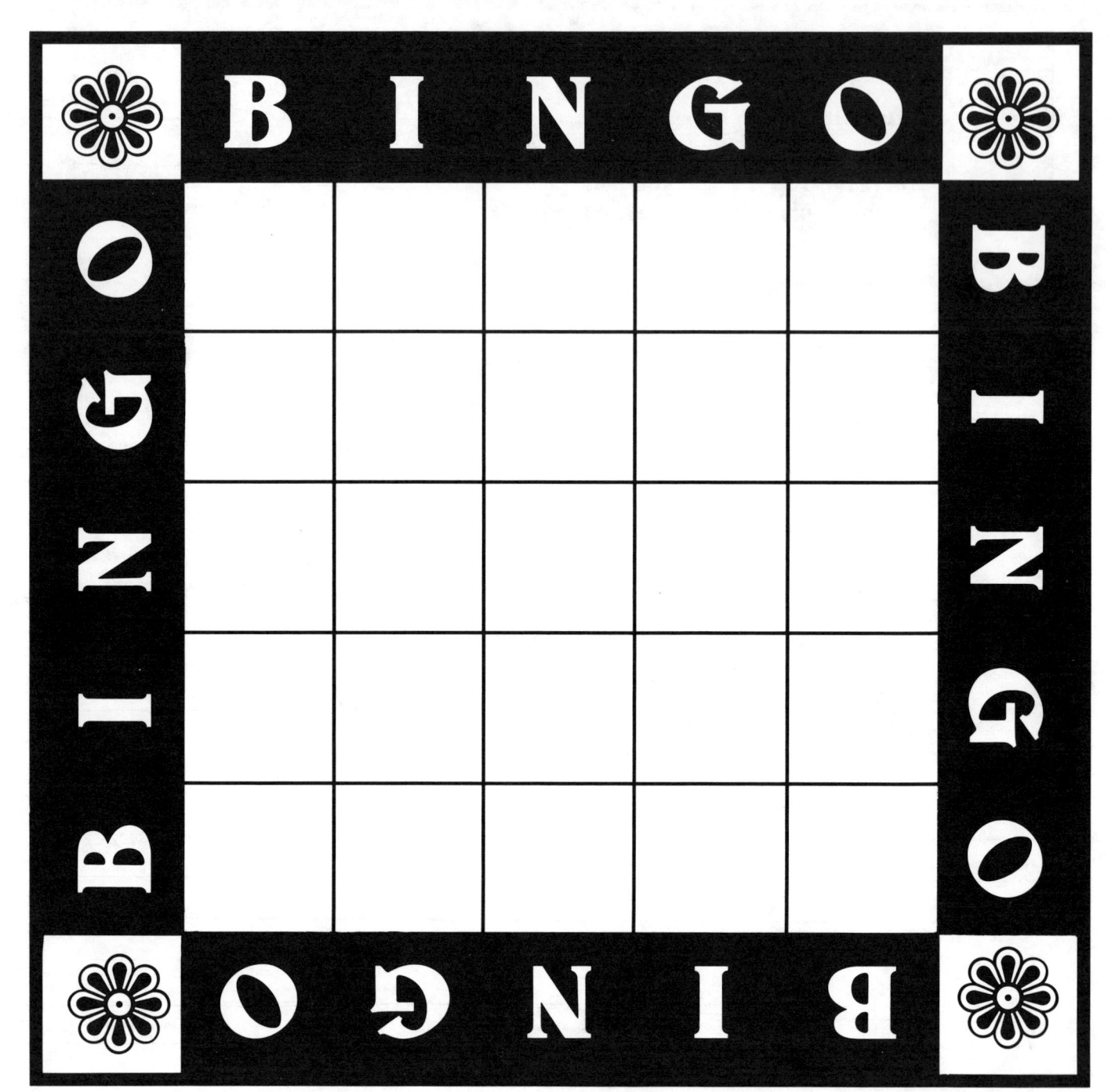

Activities

A. Oral Practice
   1. To introduce the past, the teacher writes the words *yesterday, last night, last week*, etc. on the blackboard.
   2. Each student gives a complete sentence in the simple present.
   3. Student A: *I study English everyday.* Teacher: *I studied English yesterday.*
   4. Continue until every student has participated and contributed at least one verb. After the teacher models the simple past form, other students can give it when the verb is regular.
   5. The teacher or a student can put all the verbs on the blackboard.

B. Sound and Spell*
   1. On individual 3x5 cards, write verbs in the past tense.
   2. Include verbs that end in /t/ cooked; /d/ played; /əd/ rested.
   3. Divide the class in groups. Each group gets a stack of cards.
   4. The groups sort the cards in three piles, according to their endings.

C. Regular Verb Bingo.
   1. The teacher provides the students with a list of about thirty regular verbs in the present tense. The same verbs are written on a pack of 3x5 index cards, one to a card.
   2. The students randomly fill out their bingo cards — the grid on page 80. They pick 25 verbs from their list and write them in the past tense.
   3. One of the students is chosen as the caller for each game. He or she shuffles the pack of cards and then calls out the verbs in the past tense. One of the other students or the teacher can monitor the caller's pronunciation.
   4. The students who have the called verb repeat it aloud and put a marker on their cards to cover it. Pennies make good markers.
   5. The first student to cover a horizontal, vertical, or diagonal row of five verbs calls out "Bingo" and wins the game.

References

For the Student
   1. *Side by Side, Book I*, Molinsky, Bliss, pp. 87-89, 94-96.
   2. *Grammar Exercises, Part One*, Burrows, pp. 108–112.

For the Teacher
   1. *The Grammar Book,* Celce-Murcia, Larsen-Freeman, pp. 63, 74-77.
   2. *Modern English: A Practical Reference Guide,* Frank, pp. 72-73.
   *3. *Index Card Games for ESL,* Clark, pp. 21-30.

28 Irregular past forms

Some verbs are **irregular** in the past tense. You must learn them. There is a list in the appendix.

eat — ate   **speak — spoke**   **read — read**
go — went   **know — knew**   **have — had**

*Jackie and I **ate** two bowls of Muesli yesterday.*
*They **had** a good time in Moscow last year.*

Notice the formation of questions and negative sentences.

***Did** they **have** a good time?*
*They **did not have** a good time.*

In the space below, write sentences using irregular past tense verbs.

We met Willy yesterday.
Kimiko bought a new tape.

1. _____
2. _____
3. _____
4. _____
5. _____
6. _____
7. _____
8. _____
9. _____
10. _____
11. _____
12. _____
13. _____
14. _____
15. _____

Irregular past forms *28*

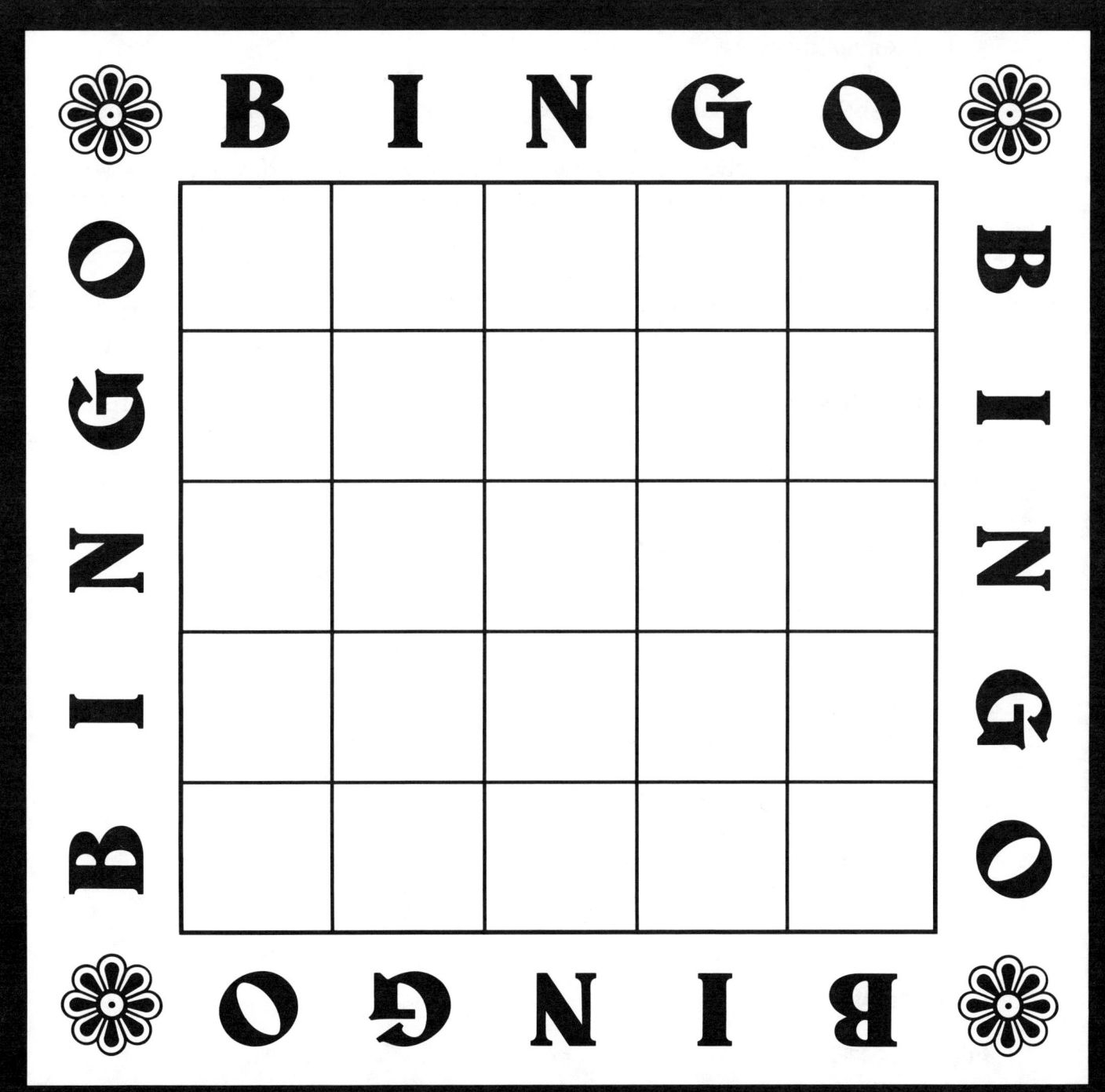

28 Irregular past forms

Activities

A. Rod Round Robin
1. With colored rods, make an intersection of Main Street.
2. Label different buildings, houses, stores, etc. with different colored rods.
3. Introduce Mr. Green (a green rod).
4. Tell a progressive story about what Mr. Green did yesterday beginning with Student A: *Mr. Green went downtown yesterday.* Student B: *He bought tennis shoes.* Whether Student B repeats Student A's sentence depends on the students' proficiency, the class size, and the time allotted for the exercise.
5. Continue the story until everybody has participated.
6. Repeat it with Mr. Black doing different things.
7. Variations: Allow each student to perfect his or her contribution and then record it.
8. If the students have been creative, the teacher may play back Mr. Green's story as a dictation. The students can then rewrite it in the simple present.

B. Matched Pairs*
1. Write 15 irregular verbs in the simple form on 15 different 3x5 cards.
2. Write 15 matching irregular verbs in the past tense.
3. Shuffle the cards and turn them face down. (See page 33.)
4. The students try to match the verb with its irregular past tense form.

C. Irregular Verb Bingo
1. Students randomly fill in the bingo card (page 83) from one of the lists of irregular verbs on page 157.
2. Follow the directions for Bingo in exercise C on page 81.

D. Chart Pattern Practice** (LAB)
1. Use the chart on page 77.
2. Teacher: *What did Joan do at 6:30?* Student: *She woke up.*
   Teacher: *What did she do after she woke up?*
3. In pairs, the students practice questions and answers in the past tense.

References

For the Student
1. *Side by Side, Book I*, Molinsky, Bliss, pp. 91-98.
2. *Grammar Exercises, Part One*, Burrows, pp. 113-118.

For the Teacher
*1. *Index Card Games for ESL*, Clark, pp. 3-20.
2. *Modern English: A Practical Reference Guide*, Frank, pp. 61-66, 72-73.
**3. *Language Teaching Techniques*, Clark, pp. 73-76.

Future — GOING TO

We <u>form</u> the future by using the verb **to be + going to**.

Singular
I **am going to** fly.
You **are going to** fly.
He, She, It **is going to** fly.

Plural
We **are going to** fly.
You **are going to** fly.
They **are going to** fly.

*Naki and Evelyn **are going to** visit Ankara.*
*Tak **is going to** study chemistry.*

Notice the formation of questions and negative sentences.

***Are** they **going to** visit Ankara?*
*They **are not going to** visit Ankara.*

In the space below, write sentences about what you are going to do tomorrow.

They are going to buy a six-pack.

1.
2.
3.
4.
5.
6.
7.
8.
9.
10.
11.
12.
13.
14.
15.
16.

29 Future — *Going to*

Dear

Your friend,

Future — GOING TO 29

Activities

A. Oral Practice
1. The teacher writes some verbs on the board — *take, write, give*, etc.
2. Teacher: *I am going to take Sally's book.* Then the teacher takes it.
3. Teacher: *I am going to write on the blackboard.* Then the teacher writes on the blackboard.
4. The teacher points to a verb on the board and a student makes a sentence and demonstrates the action.

B. Story square*

See page 21. This square is also good practice for questions: **who what, which, yes/no, how much** and tags.

C. Operation**
1. Use a cassette player, or some other similar piece of equipment.
2. Operate the cassette player, pausing before each step in the operation to state what you are going to do.

D. Oral Practice (LAB)
1. Use the activity chart on page 77.
2. Teacher: *What is Joan going to do at 6:30?* Student: *She is going to get up.*
3. In pairs, students practice questions and answers in the future.

E. Pen Pal
1. The teacher gets the names and addresses of students in another class, school, or country and gives one to each student.
2. Together the students write a class letter for practice. Encourage the use of *going to*.
3. The students write and send real letters using page 86 for rough drafts.

References

For the Student
1. *Side by Side, Book I*, Molinsky, Bliss, pp. 80-86.
2. *Grammar Exercises, Part One*, Burrows, pp. 119–122.

For the Teacher
*1. *Story Squares,* Knowles, Sasaki, pp 63-68.
**2. *ESL Operations,* Nelson, Winters.
**3. *Language Teaching Techniques,* Clark, pp. 25-30.
4. *Modern English: A Practical Reference Guide,* Frank, p. 77.

30 Future — WILL

We use **will** + the simple form of the verb to express the future.

> Ernie **will go** to school in August.
> I **will study** tonight.

Notice the formation of questions and negative sentences.

> **Will** Ernie go?
> Ernie **will not** go.

Will not is frequently contracted to **won't**.

In the space below, write sentences in the future using will.

We will drink sake.

89 Future — *WILL* 30

In the year 2020...

1. I will

2.

3.

4.

5.

*Time flees

30 Future — W*ILL*

Activities

A. Written/Oral Practice — Rod Round Robin
   1. Tell a progressive story about what Mr. Green will do tomorrow. See page 84, Activity A.
   2. Write individual stories about Mr. Green.

B. Prophesy 2020 A.D.
   1. The students write five prophesies about themselves on page 89.
   2. The teacher prepares a large piece of brown paper for each student and writes at the top, *Jorge. In the year 2020 . . .* These are posted on the walls.
   3. The students circulate and write predictions using *will* about each of their classmates.
   4. The class goes over the responses and makes corrections.

C. Chart Pattern Practice
   1. Use the Sempé cartoon on page 8.
   2. Teacher: *What will the family do next Sunday?* Student: *They will drive to the shore.*
   3. Challenge the students to see how many creative sentences they can come up with to tell the story.

References

For the Student
   1. *Side by Side, Book I*, Molinsky, Bliss, pp. 124-125.
   2. *Grammar Exercises, Part One*, Burrows, pp. 123–127.

For the Teacher
   1. *The Grammar Book,* Celce-Murcia, Larsen-Freeman, pp. 63, 74-77.
   2. *Modern English: A Practical Reference Guide,* Frank, pp. 74-75.

Imperative 31

Imperatives express a command or a request. The subject **you** is not used.

>*Close the door.*
>*Sit down.*

We use **don't** to form the negative.

>***Don't*** *close the door.*
>***Don't*** *sit down.*

Please makes imperative sentences more polite.

>***Please*** *close the door.*
>*Close the door **please**.*

In the space below, write sentences in the imperative.

Let's take a break.
Let's not have class tomorrow.

1.
2.
3.
4.
5.
6.
7.
8.
9.
10.
11.
12.
13.
14.
15.

31 Imperative

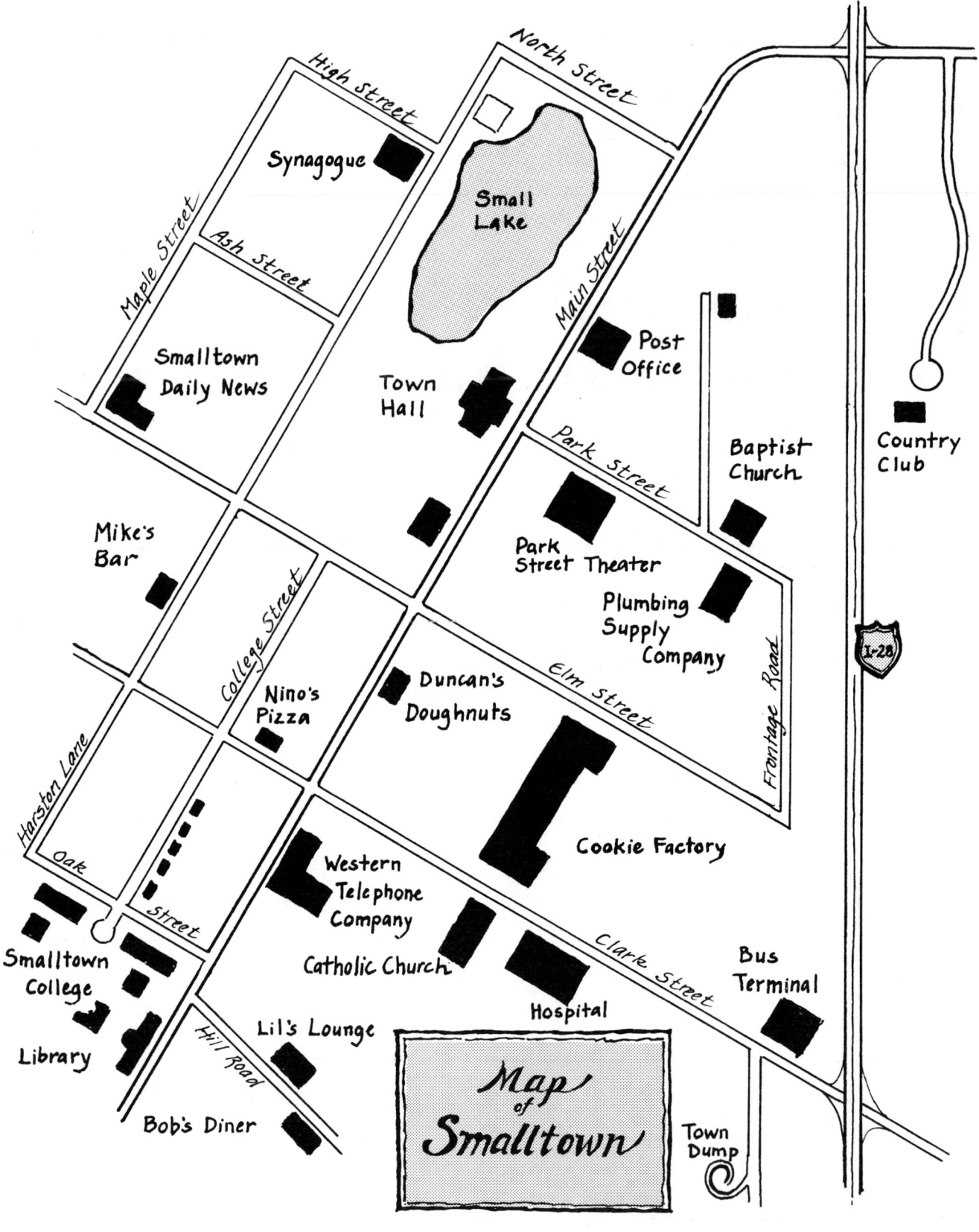

Activities

A. Operation*
   1. On individual 3 x 5 cards the teacher writes instructions on how to prepare a cup of instant coffee. For example: (Card-1). *Fill the coffee pot with water.* (Card-2). *Put the coffee pot on the stove.* Use one command per card.
   2. Scramble the cards and the students put them back in order.
   3. Prepare the coffee in class, having one student give commands from memory and another follow the directions exactly as they are given.

B. Written Practice
   1. Share a favorite recipe of yours with the class. Go over the vocabulary.
   2. Each student writes a favorite native recipe.
   3. This activity could be in preparation for a class meal.

C. Oral Practice — Where Are You?**
   1. Put a street map or road map on the board or use the map of Smalltown.
   2. One student says: *"I'm at _____. How do I get to _____?*
   3. A second student gives directions.
   4. Go out of the classroom and practice receiving and giving directions.
   5. Variation: In pairs, the students sit back to back. Student A chooses a location and says, *You are at...* A then chooses a goal and directs Student B to it. B follows the directions exactly as given with a pencil until A asks, *Where are you?*

D. TPR***
   1. The teacher gives a series of commands and the students go through the actions. For example: *Stand up. Pick up your pencil. Walk to the pencil sharpener.*
   2. When they are comfortable doing so, the students can make up and give a series of commands.

References

For the Student
   1. *Side by Side, Book I*, Molinsky, Bliss, pp. 121, 144-149.
   2. *Grammar Exercises, Part One*, Burrows, pp. 128–130.

For the Teacher
   *1. *ESL Operations*, Nelson, Winters.
   *2. *Language Teaching Techniques*, Clark, pp. 25-30.
   3. *The Grammar Book*, Celce-Murcia, Larsen-Freeman, pp. 138-141.
   4. *Modern English: A Practical Reference Guide*, Frank, pp. 57-59.
   **5. *Experiential Language Teaching Techniques*, Jerald, Clark, pp. 27-41.
   ***6. *Learning Another Language through Action*, Asher.
   ***7. *Live Action English*, Ramijn, Seely.

32 Imperative — *LET'S*

> We use **let's** to introduce requests and suggestions that involve the speaker. **Let's** is a contraction for **let us**.
>
> ***Let's** get together.*
> ***Let's** go to a movie tonight.*
>
> The negative is formed by adding **not** immediately after **let's**.
>
> ***Let's** not do that.*
> ***Let's** not go to that movie.*

In the space below, write affirmative and negative sentences using **let's**.

Let's take a break.
Let's not have class tomorrow.

1.
2.
3.
4.
5.
6.
7.
8.
9.
10.
11.
12.
13.
14.
15.
16.
17.
18.

Suggestions for our class:

1.

2.

3.

4.

5.

32 Imperative — *Let's*

Activities

A. Oral Practice — Suggestions
1. The teacher tells the students that the last part of the class is theirs.
2. On page 95 each student writes five suggestions about what he would like the class to do. Encourage practical as well as fanciful ideas.
3. The students put their favorite suggestions on the blackboard.
4. Go over the new vocabulary.
5. The class votes on what they will do.

B. Chain Drill
1. Use a list of activities such as biking, bowling, swimming, etc.* or use the chart on page 101. Let the students be inventive.
2. One student makes a suggestion. Student A: *Let's go biking*.
3. The next student says: *No, let's not. Let's play tennis*, etc.

C. Oral Practice (LAB)
1. The teacher gives the students commands. Teacher: *Speak English*.
2. The students make a request using **let's**. Student: *Let's speak English*.
3. The teacher repeats the correct request. Teacher: *Let's speak English*.
4. Repeat the activity using the negative **let's not**.

References

For the Student

Grammar Exercises, Part One, Burrows, pp. 131–134.

For the Teacher
1. *The Grammar Book,* Celce-Murcia, Larsen-Freeman, p. 142.
2. *Modern English: A Practical Reference Guide,* Frank, p. 57.
*3. *The ESL Miscellany,* Clark, Moran, Burrows, Grammar List 12 — Idioms with Go.

Polite requests 33

Would you makes a command more polite.

> *Would you open the door?*

Please makes the command very polite.

> *Would you please open the door?*
> *Would you open the door, please?*

Would you mind requires the **-ing** form of the verb.

> *Would you mind opening the door?*

Notice the response to **would you mind**.

> *No, I wouldn't* means *Yes, I will* (open the door).
> *Yes, I would* means *No, I won't* (open the door).

Shall we includes the speaker and is similar to **let's**.

> *Shall we go now?* *Yes, let's* (go).
> *No, let's not* (go).

In the space below, please write polite requests.

Would you please turn down the stereo?

1. ___
2. ___
3. ___
4. ___
5. ___
6. ___
7. ___
8. ___
9. ___
10. ___

33 Polite requests

Category \ Country	U.S.A.	JAPAN	MEXICO		
Greetings					
Visiting in the home					
Eating					
Shopping					
Dating					

Activities

A. Role Play*
   1. The students pair up.
   2. The teacher gives each pair a situation. Example: *You are in a movie theatre and the person in front of you has a big hat on. Ask him or her politely to remove the hat.*
   3. The students act out the role plays.
   4. The teacher takes notes on the mistakes.

B. Conversation
   1. In groups or as a class, fill in the grid on page 98.
   2. Discuss what is polite in America and in the students' native countries.
   3. Specific categories could be compared. Example: shopping, eating, etc.

C. Oral Practice (LAB)
   1. The teacher gives the students commands. Teacher: *Speak English.* Then cues: *would you please.*
   2. Student: *Would you please speak English?*
   3. The teacher repeats the correct response. Teacher: *Would you please speak English?*

D. The Collectors
   1. This can be a class project or a competition between two or more teams. It is a good on-going review exercise after modals have been studied.
   2. The teacher gives the students one day or the weekend to collect as many polite expressions for *please, excuse me,* and *thank you* as they can.
   3. The students list their expressions on sheets of brown paper. These are kept up for some time, and the students are encouraged to use as many different expressions as possible in class. If they learn new expressions, they can add them to their collections.

References

For the Student
   Grammar Exercises, Part One, Burrows, pp. 135–139.

For the Teacher
   *1. *Language Teaching Techniques,* Clark, p. 56.
    2. *Modern English: A Practical Reference Guide,* Frank, pp. 58, 76.

34 Modals of ability

> **Can** and **be able to** express ability.
>
> *Frank **can** eat three pizzas.*
> *Frank **is able to** eat three pizzas.*
> *I **can** finish the book.*
> *I **am able to** finish the book.*

In the space below, write sentences using **can** and **be able to**.

Jamie can bake bread.
Pam is not able to play hockey today.

1.
2.
3.
4.
5.
6.
7.
8.
9.
10.
11.
12.
13.
14.
15.
16.
17.
18.
19.
20.

Modals of ability 34

swim play tennis jog

play volleyball ski play ping pong

sail play softball ride (horses)

34 Modals of ability

Activities

A. Oral Practice
1. The teacher asks each student to tell what he can do.
2. Put the abilities on the blackboard. Example: Speak Arabic, juggle, etc.
3. In pairs, Student A asks Student B his abilities, practicing *can, be able to* with the abilities on the blackboard. Student A: *Can you speak Arabic?* Student B: *Yes, I can.* or *No, I can't.*
4. Student B can ask the questions.

B. Storysquare*

See page 21. This activity is also good practice for questions: **who**, **what**, **yes-no** questions, and tags.

C. Jazz Chants** "It's got to be somewhere," "Late again," and "I'm sorry, but."
1. The teacher explains the context and the vocabulary of the chant.
2. The students model the teacher line by line.
3. The class can be divided and the chant can be practiced in sections.

D. Chart Pattern Practice (LAB)***
1. Use the chart on page 101.
2. Practice **can** and **be able to** in statements, questions, and negatives.

References

For the Student
1. *Side by Side, Book I*, Molinsky, Bliss, pp. 74-75.
2. *Grammar Exercises, Part One*, Burrows, pp. 140–142.

For the Teacher
*1. *Story Squares,* Knowles, Sasaki, pp 21-25.
**2. *Jazz Chants,* Graham, pp. 11, 47, 61.
***3. *Language Teaching Techniques,* Clark, pp. 73-76.
4. *The Grammar Book,* Celce-Murcia, Larsen-Freeman, pp. 80-94.
5. *The ESL Miscellany,* Clark, Moran, Burrows, Grammar List 13 — Modals

Modals of permission

We use **may** and **can** to ask permission.

> **May** *I borrow your cassette?*
> **Can** *I be excused?*

Some people consider **may** to be more polite than **can**.

In the space below, write sentences using **may** and **can**.

May I have more time to finish the lesson?
Can I have dinner with you?

1. ___
2. ___
3. ___
4. ___
5. ___
6. ___
7. ___
8. ___
9. ___
10. ___
11. ___
12. ___
13. ___
14. ___
15. ___
16. ___
17. ___
18. ___
19. ___
20. ___

35 Modals of permission 104

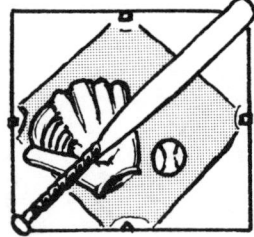

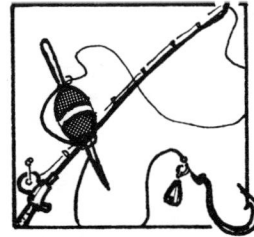

Modals of permission

Activities

A. Role Play*
1. Divide the class into groups. Each group gets a situation on a 3 x 5 card.
2. Example situations: borrow dad's car, look at a friend's dictionary, a roommate who is always borrowing clothes, etc. Students might suggest situations.
3. Each group of students writes a short dialogue.
4. The students perform their dialogues.

B. Oral Practice (LAB)
1. The teacher gives a cue, using a familiar activity such as swimming, playing golf, etc.**
2. The students respond with a request, first using **may**: *May I go swimming*.
3. a. The teacher responds with: *Yes, you may*. The students express appreciation. For example: *Great! Fantastic! Oh boy!*
   b. The teacher responds with: *No, you may not*. The students groan.
4. Alternatively, use the chart on page 101 to do a pattern practice.

C. Written Practice
1. The students send notes to each other, such as: *May I borrow your sweater?*
2. They send written responds back on the note.

D. Constructalog***
1. The students, working in pairs or small groups, write dramatic dialogues on page 104. The dramas concern one or more of the sports pictured and they should use as many polite expressions for asking permission as possible. The students perform their constructalogs.
2. Variation: The students are encouraged to use both modals of permission and ability.

References

For the Student

Grammar Exercises, Part One, Burrows, pp. 143–146.

For the Teacher

  *1. *Language Teaching Techniques*, Clark, p. 55.
 **2. *The ESL Miscellany,* Clark, Moran, Burrows, Grammar List 12 — Idioms with Go.
***3. *Language Teaching Techniques*, Clark, p. 51.
   4. *The Grammar Book*, Celce-Murcia, Larsen-Freeman, pp. 80-94.
   5. *Modern English: A Practical Reference Guide*, Frank, pp. 97-98.

36 *HAVE* and *HAVE GOT*

Have got can be used in place of **have**.

Have got

*Pam **has got** a lot of friends.*
*I **have got** a headache.*

Have

*Pam **has** a lot of friends.*
*I **have** a headache.*

This form is usually contracted in speech.

*She**'s got** a lot of friends.*
*I**'ve got** a headache.*

In the space below, write pairs of sentences using **have got** and **have**. Don't forget the contractions.

Herman has a lot of homework.
Herman's got a lot of homework.

1. _____
2. _____
3. _____
4. _____
5. _____
6. _____
7. _____
8. _____
9. _____
10. _____
11. _____
12. _____
13. _____
14. _____
15. _____
16. _____

Have ❦ Have got

1. I have the world on a string.
2. I have the whole world in my hands.
3. I have plenty of nothing.
4. I have you under my skin.
5. I have a dream.
6.
7.
8.

36 HAVE and HAVE GOT

Activities

A. Oral Practice
1. Fill a bag with assorted items.
2. Introduce **have got** with *I've got a* _____ .
3. Ask the students what they've got with them.
4. One student takes something from the bag and makes a sentence with *I've got.*
5. The next student says: *He or she's got a* _____ .

B. Oral Practice (LAB)
1. The teacher gives the students sentences with **have**. Teacher: *I have a quarter.*
2. The students change the sentences to **have got**. Student: *I've got a quarter.*
3. The teacher repeats the correct response.
4. Variation: the teacher gives each student a coin. Teacher: *Have you got a dime?* Student A: *No. I've got a nickel. Have you got a dime?* Student B: *Yes. I've got a dime. Have you got a quarter?* Student C: *No. I've got a fifty cent piece. Have you got a quarter?* . . .

C. Oral/Written Practice
1. The students take turns reading the five statements on page 107 and then changing them to use **have got**. (Meaning should be discussed because of the idioms.)
2. The students write down the statements using **have got**.
3. The teacher asks the students to add three things they **have**. For example: *I have imagination, I have a new, red Acura.*
4. Divide the blackboard into two sections — **have** and **have got**.
5. The teacher asks, *Michelle, What have you got?*, and writes some of the students' responses on the **have** side of the board.
6. First orally, and then on the board, change the **have** to **have got**. Then the students can write what they **have got** on page 107.

References

For the Student
Grammar Exercises, Part One, Burrows, pp. 147–149.

Two-word verbs — separable 37

Put on, take off, turn on, turn off, are two-word verbs that can be separated by an object.

Put on your socks. *Put your socks on.*
Take off your socks. *Take your socks off.*
Turn on the television. *Turn the television on.*
Turn off the television. *Turn the television off.*

If the object is a pronoun the verb must be separated.

*Put **them** on.*
*Turn **it** off.*

In the space below, write sentences with separable two-word verbs.

Ana Maria put her sweater on.
Ana Maria put on her sweater.
Ana Maria put it on.

1.
2.
3.
4.
5.
6.
7.
8.
9.
10.
11.
12.
13.
14.
15.

37 Two-word verbs — separable

VOCABULARY GAME

Categories:	Two-word Verbs	Verbs	Capital Cities		
P			*Paris*		
T					
S					
L					

Two-word verbs — separable

Activities

A. The Collectors
1. Assign each student the task of collecting five separable two-word verbs.*
2. On subsequent days the students share their finds. Keep a list posted.

B. Matched Pairs***
1. Write 15 two-word verbs and 15 matching definitions on 15 index cards.
2. Shuffle the cards and turn them face down.
3. The students try to match the two-word verb with the definition.

C. The News Hour**
1. Handout a list of separable two-word verbs****. The students write news stories using as many as possible. The stories can be about school or local events or about national or world affairs. One student serves as editor, another as anchor person. The News Hour can be tape recorded or video taped.**
2. Students can work together as reporter teams, planning their stories, adding two-word verbs, and editing their writing. The editor then reviews the stories and makes suggestions.
3. The class as a whole listens to or watches the tape twice. The first time is for comprehension. The second to note down all the two-word verbs used.
4. Variation: The Story Hour. The students write short stories or constructa-logs† using a list of two-word verbs. Folk tales or stories about their families are effective; add a vocabulary list on human qualities and characteristics††

D. Vocabulary Game
1. The teacher adds two categories to the chart on page 110.
2. The students, divided into teams, fill in the chart.
3. The team which finishes first with correct words wins.

References

For the Student
1. *Side by Side, Book I*, Molinsky, Bliss, pp. 73-79.
2. *Grammar Exercises, Part One*, Burrows, pp. 150-153.

For the Teacher
1. *The Grammar Book,* Celce-Murcia, Larsen-Freeman, pp. 265-279.
2. *Modern English: A Practical Reference Guide,* Frank, pp. 172-177.
*3. *Experiential Language Teaching Techniques,* Jerald, Clark, pp. 102-106.
**4. *Technology Assisted Teaching Techniques,* Duncan, pp. 32-62.
***5. *Index Card Games for ESL,* Clark, p. 3.
****6. *ESL Miscellany,* Clark, Moran, Burrows, Grammar List 14—Two-word Verbs.
†7. *Language Teaching Techniques,* Clark, pp. 51-54.
††8. *The Zodiac: Exploring Human Qualities and Characteristics,* Moore.

38 Definite article

The is a definite article. We use **the** with specific or familiar objects, persons, or incidents.

*Is **the** blue sweater yours?*
*Give me **the** old book.*

In the space below, write sentences with **the**.

The audience liked the show.
The students in this class are my friends.

1. _____
2. _____
3. _____
4. _____
5. _____
6. _____
7. _____
8. _____
9. _____
10. _____
11. _____
12. _____
13. _____
14. _____
15. _____
16. _____
17. _____
18. _____
19. _____
20. _____

Smalltown Daily

VOLUME 3   MARCH

Irish Celebrate St. Patrick's Day

DUBLIN, Ireland (UPI) — People all over Ireland celebrate Saint Patrick's Day in the traditional way. Dublin was decorated with flags and bunting. Sprigs of shamrock were for sale everywhere. They sold for thirty cents — double last year's price.

Throughout the country there were parades, pageants, sports and drama festivals, after early mass at special shrines.

Few noticed the controversy in New York, where an IRA supporter will lead the parade. The Irish want to keep their celebration apolitical.

Saint Patrick, who brought Christianity to Ireland in the fifth century, is the country's patron saint. By tradition, his feast day has been a day of celebration in Ireland.

THE MIGHTY DINOSAUR, ruler of the planet for several million years some 70 million years ago, suddenly over a relatively short period became extinct. Scientists are unsure what caused the disappearance of these big shots of earlier evolution on planet Earth.

Why Did the Dinosaurs Die?

WASHINGTON (UPI) — Scientists have disagreed for years about the cause of the extinction of dinosaurs 65 million years ago. One idea has recently received support from a group of space scientists.

They believe that the dinosaurs were killed by the effects of an asteroid smashing into the earth. They say that this huge asteroid created a giant dust cloud that blocked much of the sun's light for two or three months.

Animals, especially large ones, were more affected than plants for two reasons. First, the very low light may have made it difficult for them to find food. Second, the lower temperatures may have killed animals like the dinosaurs who could not adapt to the cold.

Coffee Probably Not Harmful

WASHINGTON (UPI) — If you drink a moderate amount of coffee, there is probably little or no threat to your health.

A new study by the American Council on Science and Health disputes claims that caffeine causes cancer, birth defects and heart disease.

"The fear of caffeine is out of proportion to its impact on health," said the director of the council. Coffee, tea, soft drinks and some other foods contain the chemical.

The study says, however, that some people who drink a large amount of coffee or tea do have problems. For example, if you drink ten cups of coffee a day, you may get headaches,

stomach aches, anxiety and sleep disturbance.

The study also says that women who are pregnant should limit their consumption. Otherwise, there may be a slight risk of birth defects.

38 Definite article

Activities

A. Written Practice (Cloze exercise)*
   1. The teacher gives the students a short paragraph leaving blanks for the definite article.
   2. The students fill in the blanks.
   3. When everybody has finished, read the paragraph aloud.

B. Oral Practice
   1. Put a variety of colored rods on the table, several rods of each color.
   2. The students practice the distinction between *give me **a** red rod* and *give me **the** red rod*.

C. Operation**
   1. Practice a familiar activity such as operating the language lab.
   2. The students put together a set of instructions, such as: *First put **the** cassette into **the** deck. Then turn **the** function knob*, etc.
   3. Use an illustrated operation.***

D. Newspaper****
   1. The students skim one of the newspaper articles on page 113 underlining the definite articles.
   2. They share lists of the definite articles they've found.
   3. They reread their chosen newspaper article and discuss it.

References

For the Student

   Grammar Exercises, Part One, Burrows, pp. 154–157.

For the Teacher

   *1. *The Grammar Book*, Celce-Murcia, Larsen-Freeman, pp. 171-188.
   2. *Modern English: A Practical Reference Guide*, Frank, pp. 125-140.
   **3. *ESL Operations*, Nelson, Winters.
   **4. *Language Teaching Techniques*, Clark, pp. 25-30.
   ***5. *Lexicarry: A Vocabulary Builder for Second Languages*, Moran, pp. 50-59.
   ****6. *Smalltown Daily: An Elementary/Intermediate/Advanced Reader*, Miller, Clark.

Indefinite article 39

A and **an** are indefinite articles. They are used with singular unspecified or unfamiliar objects, persons, or incidents.

  *I saw **a** strange dog.*
  *They had **an** accident.*

We use **an** before a word beginning with a vowel sound.

  An apple
  An artist

In the space below, write sentences with **a** and **an**.

Katrin learned a new word.

1.
2.
3.
4.
5.
6.
7.
8.
9.
10.
11.
12.
13.
14.
15.
16.
17.
18.
19.

39 Indefinite article

Activities

A. Oral/Written Practice
   1. The teacher shows the class the pictures on page 116 or a large collage of assorted fruits, vegetables, and foods. Example: an orange, an apple, a pie, bananas, eggs, etc.
   2. The students look at the picture for three minutes.
   3. Take the picture away.
   4. The students write down as many words as they can remember.
   5. One student puts the answers on the blackboard as the class calls them out.

B. Skit "The Mysterious Boy"*
   1. Read the entire skit for comprehension and go over the vocabulary.
   2. Assign two or more students to each role.
   3. Act out the skit.
   4. Variation: tape-record the skit to work on pronunciation.

C. Jazz Chant, "Friends"**
   1. The teacher explains the context and vocabulary of the chant.
   2. The students imitate the teacher line by line.
   3. The class may be divided and the chant may be practiced in sections.

References

For the Student

    Grammar Exercises, Part One, Burrows, pp. 158–161.

For the Teacher
   *1. *Skits in English as a Second Language,* Hines, p. 5.
   **2. *Jazz Chants,* Graham, p. 51.
   3. *The Grammar Book,* Celce-Murcia, Larsen-Freeman, pp. 178-184.
   4. *Modern English: A Practical Reference Guide,* Frank, pp. 125-140.

40 SOME/ANY

> **Some** is used in affirmative (+) statements.
>
> *Tim has **some** questions.*
>
> **Any** is used in negative (–) statements.
>
> *Elise doesn't have **any** questions.*
>
> **Some** and **any** are both used with questions.
>
> *Do you need **some** help?*
> *Do you need **any** help?*

In the space below, write statements and questions using **some** and **any**.

Berna needs some advice.
Do you have any gum?

1.
2.
3.
4.
5.
6.
7.
8.
9.
10.
11.
12.
13.
14.
15.
16.

Scavenger Hunt

Do you have some/any . . .

1. paper clips
2. postage stamps
3. sunglasses
4. gumdrops
5. a letter from a foreign country
6. toothbrush
7. rubber bands
8. chalk
9. pictures of your family
10. perfume

40 SOME/ANY

Activities

A. Scavenger Hunt*
   1. Have the students look at page 119 or give them a similar list.
   2. Working together as a class, define the words in the list.
   3. In pairs the students go throughout the school asking for and collecting as many of the listed objects as possible in fifteen minutes. They should be prepared to explain their mission and to ask questions using **some** and **any** where appropriate.
   4. Back in class, the students share their collections and where they got them.
   5. The students return all the objects to the owners practicing various expressions of appreciation and thanks.

B. Oral Practice
   1. Sit in a circle. Each student gets a few assorted colored rods.
   2. Teacher: *I have a blue rod and some yellow rods. Do you have any?*
   3. Student A: *I have some green rods. Do you have any?* (to Student B).
   4. Give each student a chance to tell what he has.
   5. The teacher introduces a new pattern: *Do I have any blue rods?*
   6. A variety of questions can be asked and answered by the students.

C. Oral Practice (LAB)
   1. The teacher gives a statement using **some**: *John needs some time.*
   2. The students change the statement to the negative. *John doesn't need any time.*
   3. The teacher repeats the negative statement. *John doesn't need any time.*

D. Skit, "Helpful Husband"**
   1. Read the entire skit for comprehension and go over the vocabulary.
   2. Assign two or more students to each role.
   3. Act out the skit.
   4. Variation: Perform the skit for another class.

References

For the Student
   1. *Side by Side, Book I*, Molinsky, Bliss, pp. 113, 118, 194-196.
   2. *Grammar Exercises, Part One*, Burrows, pp. 162-165.

For the Teacher
   *1. *Experiential Language Teaching Techniques*, Jerald, Clark, pp. 48-51.
   **2. *Skits in English as a Second Language*, Hines, p. 73.
   3. *The Grammar Book*, Celce-Murcia, Larsen-Freeman, pp. 178-179.
   4. *Modern English: A Practical Reference Guide*, Frank, pp. 95, 122, 123.

Demonstratives

This and **these** are used when the object is close to the speaker.

That and **those** are used when the object is some distance from the speaker.

This and **that** are singular. **These** and **those** are plural.

	Near the speaker	Some distance from the speaker
Singular	*This* desk is new.	*That* desk in the corner is new.
Plural	*These* desks are new.	*Those* desks in the corner are new.

In the space below, write sentences with **this**, **that**, **these**, **those**.

That house across the street is on fire.

1.
2.
3.
4.
5.
6.
7.
8.
9.
10.
11.
12.
13.
14.
15.
16.
17.
18.
19.

41 Demonstratives

Demonstratives

Activities

A. Jazz Chant "Selfish"*
   1. Explain the context and vocabulary of the chant.
   2. The students model the teacher line by line.
   3. The class may be divided and the chant may be practiced in sections.

B. Vocabulary Game: Parts of the Body
   1. The teacher stands in the middle of a circle with the students around her.
   2. The teacher faces a student and touches her own nose. Teacher: *This is my stomach.*
   3. The student points to the teacher's stomach. Student: *That is your stomach, and that is your nose.*
   4. The teacher continues to Student B and points to his feet and shoulders. Teacher: *Those are your feet, and those are your shoulders.*
   5. Student B touches his feet. Student B: *These are my feet, and these are my shoulders.*
   6. The teacher continues until all the students have participated.
   7. A student can come into the center and direct the activity.

C. Oral Practice (touch and point)
   1. The teacher touches an object and asks *What's this?*
   2. Student A: *It's a _____ .* Student A touches an object and asks: *What's this?* (etc.)
   3. The teacher points to an object and asks *What's that?*
   4. Student B: *It's a _____ .* Student B points to an object and asks *What's that?*.
   5. **These** and **those** can be modeled in the same way.
   6. In pairs, the students practice asking and answering similar questions. They may use the pictures of the two teams on page 122. They can write descriptions and contrasts using **this/that** and **these/those**.

References

For the Student
   1. *Side by Side, Book I*, Molinsky, Bliss, pp. 46-49.
   2. *Grammar Exercises, Part One*, Burrows, pp. 166–168.

For the Teacher
   *1. *Jazz Chants*, Graham, p. 15.
   2. *Modern English: A Practical Reference Guide*, Frank, p. 109.

42 Numbers: cardinal, ordinal

We use cardinal numbers:

1. to count

    One, two, three . . . ten, eleven.

2. to indicate quantities

    *She has **two** boyfriends.*

3. to pronounce telephone numbers and addresses.

    (215) 248-0987

We use ordinal numbers:

1. to indicate position

    *She is **first** in the class.*

2. to express the number of a day in a date.

    *May **2**, 1956 — May **second**, nineteen fifty-six*

In the space below, write sentences using cardinal and ordinal numbers.

Yesterday I ran seven miles.
This is the forty-second lesson.

1. ___
2. ___
3. ___
4. ___
5. ___
6. ___
7. ___
8. ___
9. ___
10. ___

Numbers: cardinals, ordinals

Cardinal Numbers		Ordinal Numbers	
1	one	1st	first
2	two	2nd	second
3	three	3rd	third
4	four	4th	fourth
5	five	5th	fifth
6	six	6th	sixth
7	seven	7th	seventh
8	eight	8th	eighth
9	nine	9th	ninth
10	ten	10th	tenth
11	eleven	11th	eleventh
12	twelve	12th	twelfth
13	thirteen	13th	thirteenth
14	fourteen	14th	fourteenth
15	fifteen	15th	fifteenth
16	sixteen	16th	sixteenth
17	seventeen	17th	seventeenth
18	eighteen	18th	eighteenth
19	nineteen	19th	nineteenth
20	twenty	20th	twentieth
21	twenty-one	21st	twenty-first
30	thirty	30th	thirtieth
40	forty	40th	fortieth
50	fifty	50th	fiftieth
60	sixty	60th	sixtieth
70	seventy	70th	seventieth
80	eighty	80th	eightieth
90	ninety	90th	ninetieth
100	one/a hundred	100th	one/a hundredth
101	one/a hundred (and) one	101st	one/a hundred (and) first
1,000	one/a thousand	1,000th	one/a thousandth
2,000	two thousand	2,000th	two thousandth
10,000	ten thousand	10,000th	ten thousandth
100,000	one/a hundred thousand	100,000th	one/a hundred thousandth
1,000,000	one/a million	1,000,000th	one/a millionth
1,000,000,000	one/a billion	1,000,000,000th	one/a billionth

42 Numbers: cardinals, ordinals

Activities

A. Oral/Aural Practice
  1. The teacher gives the students a ditto with a list of pairs of numbers, especially contrasting **-teen** and **-ty** and/or **-teenth** and **-tieth**. Example: 13, 30; 517, 570; 4, 14; 16th, 60th; 40, 40th, etc.
  2. The teacher says the list of numbers one by one with the students repeating. Teacher: *Thirteen*, Student: *Thirteen*, Teacher: *Thirty*, Student: *Thirty*.
  3. After all the numbers have been said by both the teacher and the students, the teacher says one number from each pair. Teacher: *Thirteen*.
  4. The students circle the number they hear.
  5. Variation: The students sit back to back. Student A says a number on his or her list (or on the list on page 125) and then either circles it or writes it down. Student B circles or writes the number he or she hears. After twelve numbers, the students compare their lists and then reverse roles.

B. Conversation*
  1. The teacher introduces the telephone and directory assistance and the phrase, *Would you please give me the number for _____ ?*
  2. Each student gets a 3x5 card with the name and city of a person.
  3. The students call the teacher (directory assistance) and ask for the number and address of the person on their card.
  4. Variation: After the students have practiced, the teacher gives them a list of five people (friends) who live in different areas of the country.
  5. The students actually call directory assistance for these numbers.

C. Game (Buzz)
  1. Choose a number (4) that will be substituted for buzz.
  2. In a circle the students begin to count and when the number 7 or any multiple of 4 comes up the student must say *Buzz*.
  3. Example: Student 1: *One*; Student 2: *Two*; Student 3: *Three*; Student 4: *Buzz*; Student 5: *Five*; etc.

References

For the Student
  1. *Side by Side, Book I*, Molinsky, Bliss, pp. 98, 99.
  2. *Grammar Exercises, Part One*, Burrows, pp. 169–173.

For the Teacher
  1. *Modern English: A Practical Reference Guide,* Frank, p. 109.
  *2. *Experiential Language Teaching Techniques,* Jerald, Clark, pp. 84-89.
  *3. *Technology Assisted Teaching Techniques,* Duncan, pp. 86-87.

43 Sequence of adjectives

Adjective word order is as follows:

Determiner	Descriptive			Adjunct	Noun
article, demonstrative, possessives	Opinion	Physical	Color		
a	lazy	fat	black		dog
this		cold	white	Vermont	winter
my	favorite	little		poetry	book

In the space below, write sentences with more than two adjectives.

Hugo saw a horrible horror movie last night.

1.
2.
3.
4.
5.
6.
7.
8.
9.
10.
11.
12.
13.
14.
15.
16.
17.
18.
19.

43 Sequence of adjectives 128

Sequence of adjectives 43

Activities

A. Written Practice
1. Make a chart on the blackboard like the one on page 127.
2. As a class write a list of determiners, descriptive adjectives, adjuncts and nouns.
3. The students write as many sentences as they can in 15 minutes with the adjectives on the board.
4. Each student reads at least one sentence.
5. Correct the sentences as a class.

B. Scrambled Sentences*
1. Write sentences with long adjective phrases and put the individual words on 3x5 cards. Example: *The huge, white, NASA space shuttle rose into the deep, blue morning sky above Florida.* Variation: write tongue twisters.
2. Scramble the cards.
3. Put the sentences back in order.
4. Variation: Start with magazine photos or illustrations from children's books in color. The students working in pairs write the sentences using as many adjectives as they can (within reason). The teacher corrects the sentences and the students put their sentences on cards to be scrambled and reconstructed by other pairs of students.

C. Oral Practice**
1. Draw a sketch on the board (or use the sketches on page 128) and ask the class: *What's this?*
2. Student A: *That's an elephant.*
3. Teacher: *Grey.*
4. Student B: *That's a grey elephant.*
5. Teacher: *Large.*
6. Student C: *That's a large, grey, elephant.* (etc.)
7. Variation: The teacher prepares one student before class to model the exercise. The students take turns drawing their choice of subjects and leading the class.

References

For the Student
   Grammar Exercises, Part One, Burrows, pp. 174–179.

For the Teacher
   *1. *Index Card Games For ESL,* Clark, p. 31.
   **2. *The Grammar Book,* Celce-Murcia, Larsen-Freeman, pp. 390-399.
   3. *Modern English: A Practical Reference Guide,* Frank, pp. 114-116.

44 Nationality

Proper nouns and adjectives referring to nationalities always begin with a capital letter. There are many irregular forms.

Country	Person	Adjective
Honduras	Honduran	Honduran
Israel	Israeli	Israeli
France	Frenchman	French

*Napoleon is from **Honduras***
*She is an **Israeli**.*
*Is that **French** perfume?*

In the space below, write sentences about your classmates.

The two Japanese students are from Tokyo.
That Russian spoke both French and English.

1.
2.
3.
4.
5.
6.
7.
8.
9.
10.
11.
12.
13.
14.
15.
16.

Nationality 44

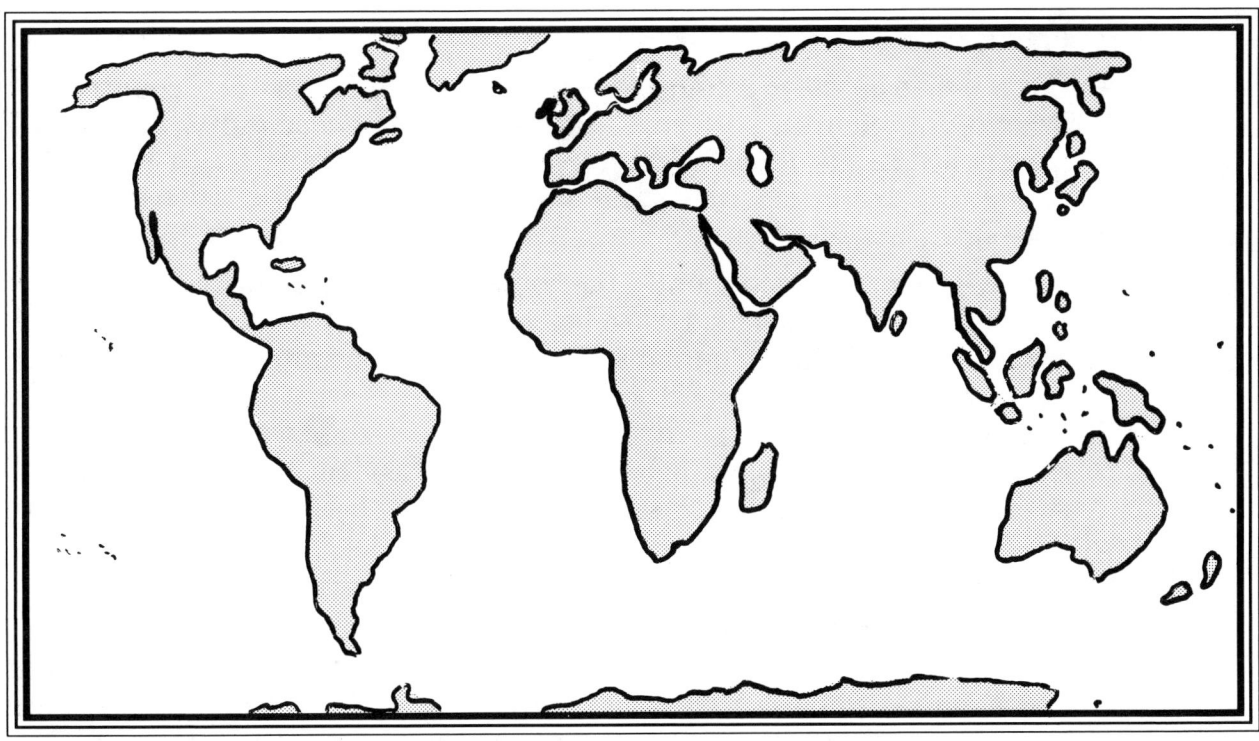

44 Nationality

Activities

A. Oral Practice*
1. Use the map on the preceding page to locate and name several countries.
2. Practice the following pattern: *Senegal is here. Mamadou is from Senegal. He is a Senegalese. He is Senegalese.*

B. Conversation*
1. Write the names of each country represented in your class on the blackboard.
2. Discuss what a custom is. Give a few examples.
3. The students take a few minutes to think about some interesting customs in their own cultures.
4. In pairs, the students explain their customs to each other.
5. Come together as a group and have each pair of students explain each other's customs to the rest of the class.

C. Written Practice
1. Write short compositions titled A _____Custom.
2. Variation: The students each take a composition (not their own) and present the custom to the class in their own words. The other students can ask questions. If the presenter does not know the answer, he asks the author and then tells the class.

D. Interviews/Oral Practice (See Pages 17-18)
1. Focus the interviews on the following questions: *What is your name? Where are you from? What language do you speak? What is your favorite kind of food?*
2. The students may question each other in pairs or in a large group.

References

For the Student
1. *Side by Side, Book I*, Molinsky, Bliss, pp. 52-54.
2. *Grammar Exercises, Part One*, Burrows, pp. 180–183.

For the Teacher
*The ESL Miscellany, Clark, Moran, Burrows, Grammar List 3, Nationality Words.

45 Comparative constructions

To form the comparative:

We add **-er** to all one-syllable adjectives.

> old — old**er**
> young — young**er**

We place **more** or **less** before adjectives that have three or more syllables.

> important — **more** important, **less** important
> intelligent — **more** intelligent, **less** intelligent

Two-syllable adjectives follow either rule. In general, adjectives ending in **-ful, -ous, -ish, -ed, -ing** take **more**.

> doubtful — **more** doubtful
> selfish — **more** selfish

Two-syllable adjectives ending in **y** usually take **er**.

> pret**ty** — prett**ier** (note that **y** becomes **i**).

Good and **bad** are irregular.

> good — better
> bad — worse

Comparatives are followed by **than**.

> *Katie is old**er than** Michael.*
> *My homework is **more** important **than** the party.*

In the space below, write sentences comparing members of your family.

I am taller than my sister.

1. _____
2. _____
3. _____
4. _____
5. _____
6. _____

45 Comparative constructions

134

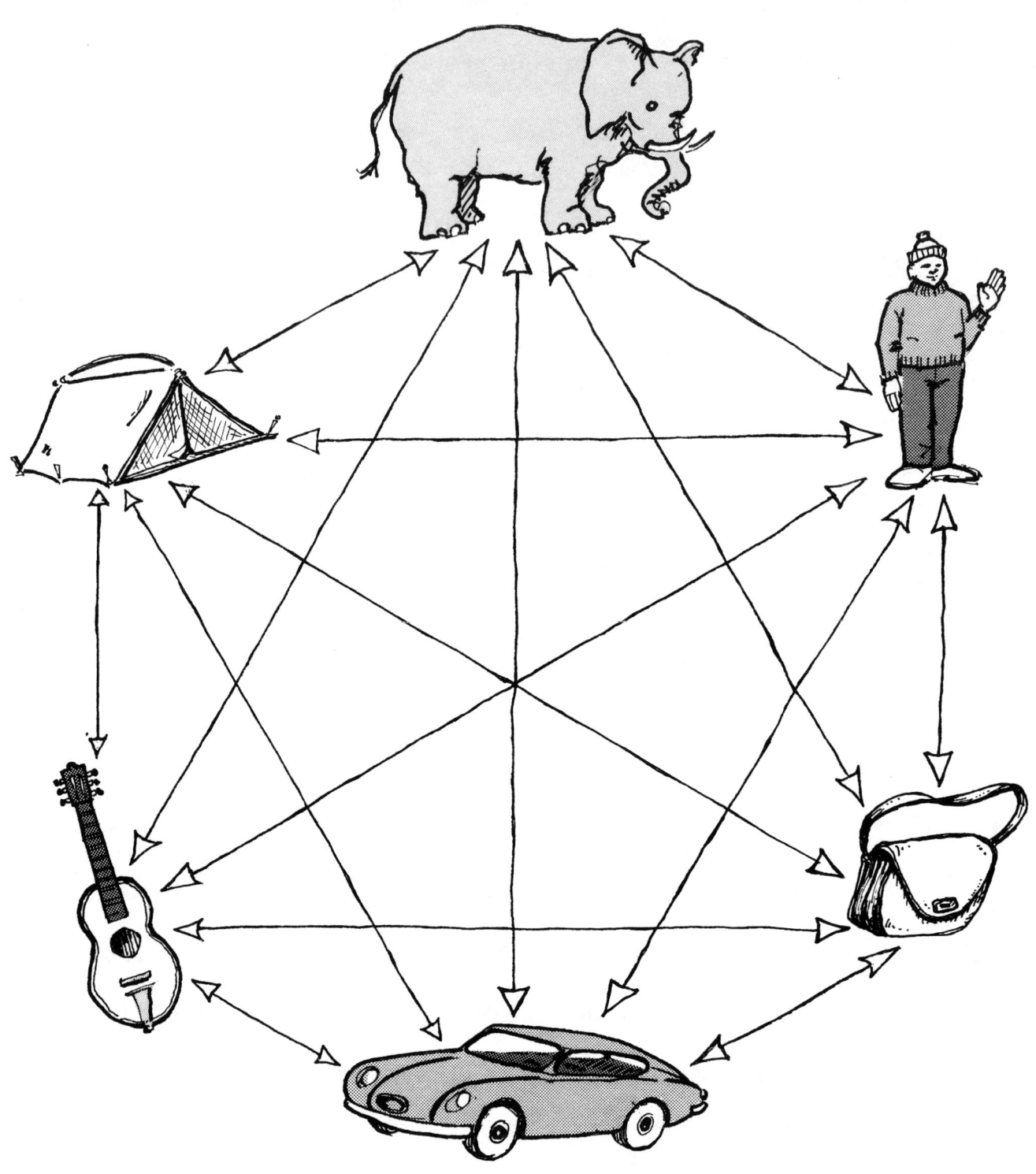

Comparative constructions   *45*

Activities

A. Oral Practice
1. Two students stand in front of the class.
2. The class makes comparisons.
3. The teacher writes the adjectives on the blackboard.
4. After each student has participated go over the vocabulary and spelling.
5. In pairs the students write five comparative sentences about any two students in the class. Example: *Mutlaq is more serious than Alejandro.*
6. Variation: Change comparative sentences to questions and have each pair ask the class one question. Example: *Who is more serious than Alejandro?*

B. Circus Brainstorming Game
1. The teacher divides the class into two teams and gives them a time limit.
2. The teams study the picture on page 134 and then brainstorm and write down as many complete comparative sentences as time allows.
3. As a class, the students review and approve the sentences. The team with the most correct sentences wins.

C. Written Practice
1. The students write sentences or a short paragraph comparing two places they have lived in, or their hometown and where they are living now.
2. Variation: Use one of the students' paragraphs as a lab dictation.

D. Conversation*
1. Choose a topic, such as academic subjects.
2. Each student contributes a sentence comparing two subjects. Example: *Business is more practical than history.*
3. Discuss the various points of view expressed.

References

For the Student
1. *Side by Side, Book I,* Molinsky, Bliss, pp. 130-131, 135.
2. *Grammar Exercises, Part One,* Burrows, pp. 184–187.

For the Teacher
1. *The Grammar Book,* Celce-Murcia, Larsen-Freeman, pp. 491-500.
2. *Modern English: A Practical Reference Guide,* Frank, pp. 118-121.
*3. *Language Teaching Techniques,* Clark, pp. 59-62.

46 Superlative constructions

To form the superlative:

We add **-est** to all one-syllable adjectives.

old — old**est**
young — young**est**

We place **most** before all adjectives that have three or more syllables.

important — **most** important
intelligent — **most** intelligent

The is placed before all superlatives.

*Mary Carmen is **the** old**est** student in the class.*
*This is **the most** important news.*

Two-syllable adjectives follow either rule. See p. 133.

Good and **bad** are irregular.

good — best
bad — worst

In the space below, write sentences using the superlative forms.

Panama City is the most beautiful city in the world.
Ouagadougu is the biggest city in Upper Volta.

1. _____
2. _____
3. _____
4. _____
5. _____
6. _____
7. _____
8. _____

46 Superlative constructions

Visit _____.

It's the most!
Come and see for yourself.
You'll love it.

Our chosen tourist spot:

Things to See	Things to Do	Adjectives

46 Superlative constructions

Activities

A. Written/Oral Practice*
   1. The students write a TV commercial.
   2. Choose between three products. Example: *Sparkles toothpaste, for the shiniest teeth in town. Kleeno detergent, for the cleanest clothes in town. Ezgo for the most powerful gasoline.*
   3. For more structured commercials, refer to the footnote.
   4. Have the students perform their commercials for the class.

B. Game (College Bowl)
   1. Divide the class into three teams, (1, 2, 3).
   2. Prepare 30 questions of interest in the superlative. Example: *What is the largest ocean in the world?*
   3. Ask the question and the team member who raises his or her hand first must answer with a full sentence.
   4. If a team member raises a hand before the question is finished, stop there. They must answer.
   5. The team gets ten points for a correct answer.
   6. If they miss the remaining teams compete. They get five points for a correct answer.

C. Oral Practice (See Page 135, Activities A and D)
   Follow the same procedure using superlative forms.

D. Travel Brochure
   1. The class chooses a popular tourist spot they all know and fills in the chart on page 137. Example: Sears Tower, Epcot Center, Old Quebec.
   2. In groups, the students write and illustrate travel brochures about their spot. They should use at least five superlatives.
   3. Variation: Collect travel brochures and list sentences with superlatives.

References

For the Student
   1. *Side by Side, Book I*, Molinsky, Bliss, pp. 138-142.
   2. *Grammar Exercises, Part One*, Burrows, pp. 188-191.

For the Teacher
   *1. *Technology Assisted Teaching Techniques*, Duncan, p. 51.
   *2. *Side by Side, Book II*, Molinsky, Bliss, p. 112.
   3. *The Grammar Book*, Celce-Murcia, Larsen-Freeman, pp. 508-518.
   4. *Modern English: A Practical Reference Guide,* Frank, pp. 118-121.

Quantity words   47

We use **much, a little,** and **less** with non-count nouns.*

> How **much** money do you need?
> This plant needs **a little** water.
> I need **less** time to study today.

We use **many, a few** and **fewer** with count nouns.

> How **many** chairs are in the classroom.
> I have **a few** dollars.
> There are **fewer** students in our class.

* See page 37, non-count nouns.

In the space below, write sentences using quantity words.

I take a little sugar with my coffee.
Class will be over in a few minutes.

1.
2.
3.
4.
5.
6.
7.
8.
9.
10.
11.
12.
13.
14.
15.

47 Quantity words

Guacamole from Mexico
(Avocado Dip)

This is one of my favorite recipies. It is based on Diana Kennedy's recipe in *The Cuisines of Mexico*.

Grind a little finely chopped onion, one or two fresh, green *chilies serranos*, two sprigs of fresh corriander, and a good pinch of salt. Make a smooth paste.

Mash the flesh of two medium avocados (about two cups) with the 1/3 cup of chili/onion paste.

Chop up one large tomato (about one pound), a few more tablespoons of chopped onion and a couple more sprigs of finely chopped corriander.

Mix the tomato into the *guacamole* and serve immediately. If you have to wait more than a few minutes, put the avocado seed in the *guacamole* and sprinkle a few drops of lime juice on top.

Serve the dip with a few warm *tortillas* or a bowl of *taco* chips.

¡Buen provecho!
Andrés

My Favorite Recipe from _____

Activities

A. Written Practice (See Page 39, Activity B)

The students choose to talk about their school in their home country or the community where they are studying. After the blackboard is full of non-count nouns, the students write about their hometowns.

B. Skit, "Patience"*
   1. Read the entire skit for comprehension and go over the vocabulary.
   2. Assign two or more students to each role.
   3. Act out the skit.

C. Operation Omelette or Tea**
   1. The students study either of the illustrated operations and write detailed descriptions using as many quantity words as possible. They then compare their work; one student lists all the quantity expressions on brown paper.
   2. Variation: In pairs, the students plan and record descriptions of the operations using quantity works. The pairs exchange recordings and do the operations exactly as instructed on tape.
   3. For followup, pairs of students go to the cafeteria. Student A tells Student B how much of what he or she wants. Student B orders.

D. Delights
   1. This is a good exercise for students who like to cook. One or two of them read over the recipe on page 140. They discuss it to be sure they understand it.
   2. The rest of the class then tries to learn how to make quacamole by asking questions. The cooks only explain what they are asked.
   3. Interested students then volunteer to write their own favorite recipes, and the class questions them in the same way.

References

For the Student
   1. *Side by Side, Book I*, Molinsky, Bliss, pp. 114, 115, 121.
   2. *Grammar Exercises, Part One*, Burrows, pp. 192–194.

For the Teacher
   *1. *Skits in English as a Second Language*, Hines, pp. 93-97.
   **2. *Lexicarry: A Vocabulary Builder for Second Language*, Moran, pp. 57, 50.
   3. *Modern English: A Practical Reference Guide*, Frank, pp. 123-124, 138.
   4. *The Grammar Book*, Celce-Murcia, Larsen-Freeman, pp. 189-202.

48 Adverbs of manner

We form adverbs of manner by adding an **ly** to adjectives.

Adjective	**Adverb**
soft	soft**ly**
quick	quick**ly**

Adverbs of manner tell how something is done.

*Sayuri speaks soft**ly**.*
*Justin learns quick**ly**.*

In the space below, write sentences with adverbs of manner.

My roommate eats noisily.
I can do this lesson easily.

1.
2.
3.
4.
5.
6.
7.
8.
9.
10.
11.
12.
13.
14.
15.
16.
17.

Adverbs of manner

48 Adverbs of manner

Activities

A. Scrambled Sentences*

1. Write sentences that include adverbs, putting each word on an individual 3x5 card.
2. Scramble the cards.
3. Put the sentences back in order, trying to make as many variations as possible with each sentence by putting the adverbs in different places.
4. Have the students write the sentences. See page 129, Lesson 43B.

B. Game

1. Send one student out of the room. That student must guess the adverb.
2. The class decides on an adverb. Example: *quickly*.
3. The student returns and asks the class members questions. Example: *What's your name? Where are you from?* etc.
4. The class members answer quickly.
5. The student continues asking questions until he or she can guess the adverb.

C. Oral Practice (LAB)

1. The students answer questions with one word.
2. Teacher: *How does a soft speaker speak?* Student: *Softly*.
3. Teacher: *How does a graceful dancer dance?* Student: *Gracefully*.

D. Cartoon

1. In pairs, the students write captions for the cartoon on page 143. They must use at least three adverbs of manner.
2. They share the cartoons with the class.
3. Variation: The students take turns describing the Sempé cartoon on page 146, using as many adverbs of manner as possible. One student lists the adverbs on the board.

References

For the Student

1. *Side by Side, Book I*, Molinsky, Bliss, pp. 152-153.
2. *Grammar Exercises, Part One*, Burrows, pp. 195–198.

For the Teacher

*1. *Index Card Games for ESL*, Clark, p. 31.
2. *Modern English: A Practical Reference Guide*, Frank, pp. 141-162.

Adverbs of frequency

The adverbs of frequency tell us generally how many times an action occurs.

Adverb	% of action	
always	100%	I **always** do my homework.
usually	80-90%	She **usually** jogs after class.
*sometimes	40-50%	**Sometimes** they speak Arabic.
never	0%	He **never** works on the weekend.

Adverbs of frequency generally come before the main verb.

*She **never eats** meat.*

They generally come after the verb **to be**.

*He **is never** late for class.*

***Sometimes** is often used at the beginning or the end of a sentence.*

***Sometimes** I go to the movies alone.*
*I go to the movies alone **sometimes**.*

In the space below, write sentences using **always, usually, sometimes** and **never**. Watch your word order!

Nancy never scuba dives alone.
Patrick usually runs three miles a day.

1. _____
2. _____
3. _____
4. _____
5. _____
6. _____
7. _____
8. _____

49 Adverbs of frequency

1

2

3

4

5

6

Playing house

Adverbs of frequency   49

Activities

A. Oral Practice (See pp. 71-72)

The teacher asks the students questions about their daily habits, while referring to the activity chart on page 77. The teacher and students use as many adverbs of frequency as possible in their questions and answers.
Teacher: *What time do you usually get up?*

B. Written/Oral Practice — Scrambled Paragraphs*
1. Each student writes a short paragraph about his or her daily activities including adverbs of frequency.
2. If there are ten students in the class there should be ten sentences in the paragraph. If the class is larger, divide into groups.
3. Cut each story in sentence strips. Mix up the order of the sentences.
4. The teacher gives each student a sentence and gives them one minute to memorize it.
5. The teacher collects the strips.
6. The class must reconstruct the story. Use the blackboard if necessary.

C. Written Practice — Sempé
1. Each student writes a story about *Playing House* by Sempé. It should include at least 4 adverbs of frequency. Share the stories with the class.
2. Variation: Round Robin. Each student starts a description of *Playing House* and then passes the story on to the next student. The students try to put one adverb of manner or frequency in each sentence. Add ten or more sentence to each story. Post the finished stories.

D. Oral Practice (LAB)
1. Teacher: *Omar walks to school. Usually.*
2. Student: *Omar usually walks to school.*
3. Teacher: *Omar usually walks to school.*
4. Student echoes: *Omar usually walks to school.*
5. Teacher: *Mohab is a good student. Always.*
6. Student: *Mohab is always a good student.* etc.

References

For the Student
1. *Side by Side, Book I*, Molinsky, Bliss, pp. 63, 68, 70-71.
2. *Grammar Exercises, Part One*, Burrows, pp. 199-202.

For the Teacher
1. *The Grammar Book,* Celce-Murcia, Larsen-Freeman, pp. 203-217.
2. *The ESL Miscellany,* Clark, Moran, Burrows, p. 38.
*3. *Index Card Games for ESL*, Clark, pp. 31-46.

50 Prepositions of time

> Notice the sequence of specific to general.
>
> **Time — at, on, in**
>
> Class starts **at** 8:30 sharp. (specific)
> Class starts **on** Friday.
> Class starts **in** June. (general)
>
> **Dates — on, in**
>
> I was born **on** April 16, 1955. (specific)
> I was born **in** April. (general)

In the space below, write sentences with **at, on, in,** practicing time and dates.

The test begins at 2:30.
Anders was born on September 15.

1.
2.
3.
4.
5.
6.
7.
8.
9.
10.
11.
12.
13.
14.
15.
16.

Prepositions of time 50

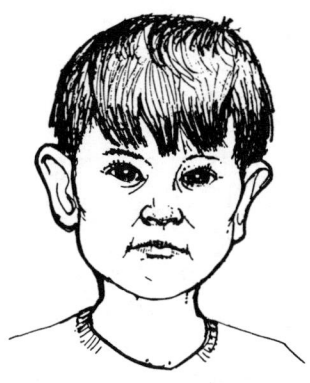

50 Prepositions of time

Activities

A. Oral Practice
   1. Refer to the daily activity chart on page 77 or page 101.
   2. Variation: Make up and hand out a schedule of daily activities with the times given. Refer to lists on pages 158 to 160 and/or other lists of cooking, eating, housekeeping, recreation, sports, business, or education vocabulary for suggestions.*
   3. Practice questions and answers using as many prepositions of time as possible. The teacher models: *When do you go jogging? Do you jog on Fridays? In January?*
   4. The teacher writes the responses on the board and turns the questioning over to the students.

B. Written Practice
   1. The teacher shows the class the pictures on page 149 and asks enough questions about one of them to start the creative process.
   2. The students write a short story or sentences about one of the characters.
   3. Stories should include where the character lives, what he does, his routine schedules, when he was born.
   4. The students share stories with each other.
   5. Variation: Use one of the short stories as a dictation in the language laboratory.

C. Written Practice — Personal Histories
   1. Create a few short paragraphs about yourself.
   2. Leave out the prepositions and have the students fill them in.
   3. Example: *I was born _____ Tegucigalpa _____ May 18, 1956. I was born _____ 3:00 a.m.*
   4. Variation: Each student creates a short paragraph about him or herself and leaves the prepositions out. The students switch papers and fill in the blanks.

References

For the Student
   1. *Grammar Exercises, Part One,* Burrows, pp. 203–207.

For the Teacher
   1. *The Grammar Book,* Celce-Murcia, Larsen-Freeman, pp. 250-261.
   2. *Modern English: A Practical Reference Guide,* Frank, pp. 163-165.
   *3. *The ESL Miscellany,* Clark, Moran, Burrows, Topics Lists.

Prepositions of place and position 51

Notice the sequence of specific to general with addresses:

*I live **at** 711 Harston Lane.* (specific)
*I live **on** Harston Lane.*
*I live **in** Philadelphia.*

Other prepositions of place and position are:

near	**under**	**on**
by	**in**	**over**
beside	**against**	**between**

In the space below, write sentences using prepositions of place and position. Describe your classroom.

Marcia lives in Rio de Janeiro
Ingrid's dictionary is under her desk.

1.
2.
3.
4.
5.
6.
7.
8.
9.
10.
11.
12.
13.
14.
15.
16.

51 Prepositions of place and position

Prepositions of place and position

Activities

A. Oral Practice
1. The teacher writes prepositions on the blackboard.
2. With rods, the teacher demonstrates each preposition and asks for a student to give a sentence. Student: *The red rod is against the blue rod.*
3. When all the prepositions have been demonstrated with the rods, the teacher sits back to back with a student volunteer.
4. Each person gets a matched set of assorted colored rods.
5. Give commands, and try to construct the same building. Teacher: *Put a blue rod next to a green rod. Put a yellow rod on the green rod.* etc.
6. Break the students into pairs and have them do the same.

B. Oral Practice
1. The teacher draws a large picture of a lake, a house, trees, a hammock between the trees, a canoe in the lake, etc.
2. One student goes to the blackboard. He or she must not see the picture.
3. The teacher shows the class the picture. They give commands so the student at the blackboard can draw the exact picture.
4. Variation: The students sit back to back. One student gives commands: *Draw a tree. Draw a house beside the tree.* etc.
5. Both the students should follow the commands. Do the pictures come out the same?

C. Written Practice
1. The students each write a description of the picture on page 152. In pairs they compare and correct their work.
2. The students describe in detail their dorm rooms or their rooms at home. They switch papers and draw maps or pictures of each other's rooms. They discuss the results.
3. Variation: A student description can be used as a dictation in the language laboratory.

References

For the Student
1. *Side by Side, Book I,* Molinsky, Bliss, pp. 36, 144-149.
2. *Grammar Exercises, Part One,* Burrows, pp. 208–212.

For the Teacher
1. *The Grammar Book,* Celce-Murcia, Larsen-Freeman, pp. 250-261.
2. *Modern English: A Practical Reference Guide,* Frank, pp. 165-168.

52 Prepositions of direction

> The following prepositions show direction. They are often used with verbs of motion.
>
> | | |
> |---|---|
> | **Into** | I walked **into** the class. |
> | **Toward** | Walk **toward** the post office. |
> | **Out of** | The dog ran **out of** the burning building. |
> | **From** | It came **from** outer space. |

In the space below, write sentences with **into, toward, out of** and **from**.

I bumped into Mustafa this morning.
Why did he walk out of the class?

1.
2.
3.
4.
5.
6.
7.
8.
9.
10.
11.
12.
13.
14.
15.
16.
17.
18.
19.

Prepositions of direction

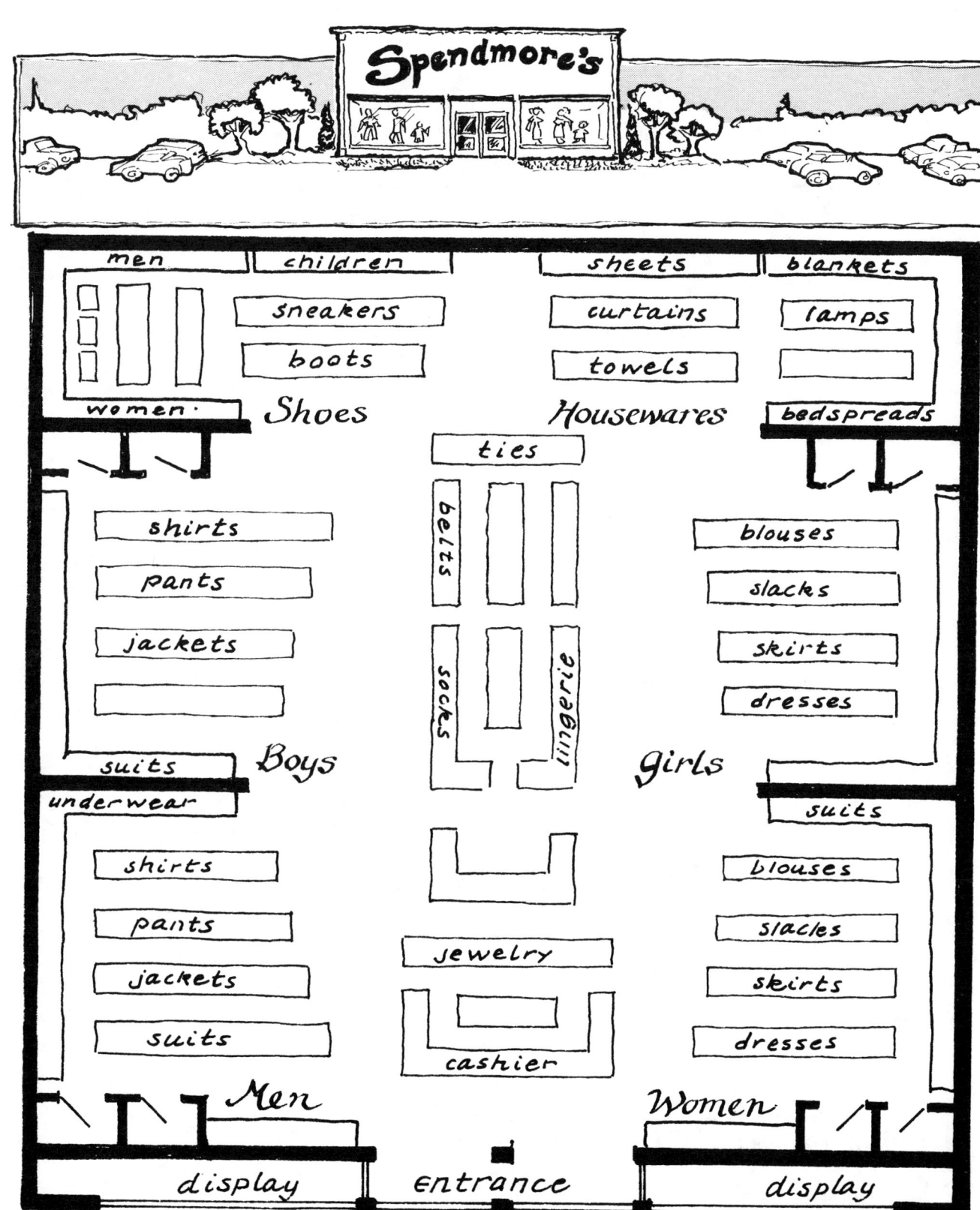

52   Prepositions of direction

Activities

A. The Collectors
1. The class is divided into pairs. Each team is given five to ten minutes to think of all the prepositions of direction they can and write sentences for each.
2. The teacher can ask which team has the most. One of those students then writes on a piece of brown paper. The other students volunteer prepositions and everyone reads their sentences using them.
3. Keep the paper posted and add to it as students collect more prepositions.

B. Written Practice
1. As a class, write a step-by-step description on the blackboard of how to go from the class to a familiar point on campus or near the school.
2. Each student writes individual directions from the classroom to their dorm room or someplace else near the school.
3. Exchange papers and follow the directions on your paper.
4. Come back together and share experiences.

C. Oral Practice
1. The teacher recommends to the class a favorite restaurant and explains how to get there.
2. In pairs, the students recommend a favorite restaurant to each other and give directions.
3. Variation: The students can be taped and transcripts can be written. The students can then correct their mistakes.

D. Oral Practice
1. The teacher uses the map of the inside of a large department store on page 155 or gives the class copies of a map of the city or a downtown section.
2. The students sit back to back. Student A gives Student B directions from a known starting point to a certain location. Student B must follow directions and arrive at the same place.
5. When Student A is finished, Student B gives directions.

References

For the Student
1. *Side by Side, Book I*, Molinsky, Bliss, pp. 144-149.
2. *Grammar Exercises, Part One*, Burrows, pp. 213–217.

For the Teacher
1. *The Grammar Book,* Celce-Murcia, Larsen-Freeman, pp. 250-261.
2. *Modern English: A Practical Reference Guide,* Frank, pp. 166-168.

Appendix

Irregular verbs

Present	Past	Present	Past
be	was/were	make	made
become	became	meet	met
begin	began	owe	owed
blow	blew	pay	paid
bring	brought	put	put
build	built	quit	quit
catch	caught	read	read
come	came	ride	rode
cost	cost	run	ran
do	did	say	said
drink	drank	see	saw
drive	drove	sell	sold
eat	ate	send	sent
fall	fell	shake	shook
feed	fed	shut	shut
feel	felt	sing	sang
fight	fought	sit	sat
find	found	sleep	slept
fly	flew	speak	spoke
forget	forgot	stand	stood
get	got	steal	stole
give	gave	sweep	swept
go	went	swim	swam
grow	grew	take	took
have	had	teach	taught
hear	heard	tell	told
hit	hit	think	thought
hold	held	throw	threw
hurt	hurt	wear	wore
keep	kept	weep	wept
know	knew	win	won
lay	laid	write	wrote
lead	led		
leave	left		
lend	lent		
light	lit		
lose	lost		

Word groups

Agriculture

field
barn
farm
crop
insecticide
dairy
cattle
poultry
to cultivate
to plant
to raise
to harvest

Aviation

airline
aircraft
jet
propeller
hangar
pilot
mechanic
instrument
altitude
radar
to land
to take off

Automobile

model
tires
brakes
transmission
driver
passenger
compact
engine
to repair
to rent
to drive
to speed

Banks

account
check
interest
teller
savings
statement
loan
overdrawn
to deposit
to withdraw
to cash
to bounce

Business

employee
employer
executive
owner
private
public
gross
net
fiscal
to invest
to buy
to sell

Computers

hardware
software
data
display
disk
print-out
memory
electronic
input
to store
to manipulate
to operate

Education

system
elementary
secondary
college
course
undergraduate
degree
to enroll
to register
to attend
to drop out
to graduate

Employment

job
occupation
career
position
union
contract
benefits
to apply
to work
to hire
to quit
to fire

Energy

electricity
fuel
nuclear
petroleum
power
solar
passive
plant
to pollute
to consume
to conserve
to generate

Family

mother
father
sister
brother
aunt
uncle
cousin
grandparent
relative
younger
older
to marry

Health

hospital
clinic
patient
nurse
physician
injection
operation
fever
aspirin
to ache
to cough
to prescribe

Mathematics

addition
subtraction
division
multiplication
solution
sum
algebra
trigonometry
fraction
to equal
to solve
to calculate

Food

vegetable
fruit
bread
meat
dairy product
dessert
fish
sweet
bitter
to cook
to bake
to taste

Laundry

washer
drier
detergent
bleach
dirty
clean
wrinkled
damp
to load
to dry
to fold
to iron

Music

artist
album
record
concert
jazz
rock
classical
piano
guitar
to sing
to compose
to play

Geography

north
south
east
west
coast
desert
plains
island
valley
mountain
river
ocean

Literature

author
critic
novel
poem
short story
play
romantic
realistic
classic
to publish
to recite
to perform

Newspaper

reporter
editor
headline
editorial
classified
comics
column
edition
to report
to advertise
to investigate
to scan

Word groups

Photography
camera
film
flash
lens
slide
snapshot
exposure
setting
to develop
to print
to enlarge
to process

Restaurant
waiter
waitress
host
hostess
menu
tip
hungry
delicious
inexpensive
to order
to reserve
to take out

Travelling
tourist
travel agent
guide
route
itinerary
map
guidebook
accomodations
reservations
to hitchhike
to tour
to visit

Politics
candidate
governor
mayor
senator
voter
party
election
majority
conservative
liberal
to elect
to vote

Softball
ball
bat
glove
base
infield
outfield
safe
out
to pitch
to catch
to run
to hit

Vegetation
tree
plant
bush
flower
garden
park
blossom
foliage
to grow
to plant
to prune
to weed

Recreation
sports
camping
hiking
boating
swimming
skiing
outdoor
amateur
to play
to watch
to attend
to participate

Television
set
channel
cable
program
show
commercial
entertaining
boring
to watch
to televise
to turn on
to enjoy

Weather
rain
snow
fog
wind
mild
humid
temperature
cloudy
sunny
hazy
to cloud up
to clear

Interplay

Interplay is a label for our approach to language learning and teaching. As the word "play" suggests, the label itself should not be taken too seriously. *Interplay* is most emphatically not "the new method" based on new scientific evidence or proven effective in 9 out of 10 language classrooms. It is neither a revolution nor a final solution. We offer the term only as a convenient and appropriate label for some ideas and practices which have proven to be useful and effective.

The first half of *Interplay*, the prefix "inter," suggests that we see language learning and even language itself as a fundamentally social activity to which movement, interaction, and give-and-take are vital. Just as it takes two hands to clap, it takes two humans to communicate. This social aspect of language cannot be neglected whether we are talking about pedagogy or methodology, curricula or materials.

Constant and genuine give-and-take interaction should be a basic principle for both language teachers and learners, and although space does not permit us to expand on this particular conclusion or its application, the most significant word is "genuine." For give-and-take interactions to be genuine, the giving and taking must be in two directions. In practical terms, all give and no take too often results in all teach and no learn.

The other half of our label is "play" and we are, ultimately, serious about that. We think language learning and teaching should involve signficant amounts of play; after all, we certainly learned a lot of our native language in the context of "playing." Not every moment of class should involve games, songs, skits and fun, laughing, joking and fooling around, but we have come to the conclusion that language learning and teaching is most successful where the prevailing mood is light and cooperation and relaxation prevail over competition and stress.

Earlier we said that *Interplay* is not a new method. Our pedagogy can best be described as eclectic. We think that there is a time and place for practically every known kind of teaching practice, whether it be a rigid structure drill or an informal discovery procedure. There is a time and place for memorizing lists as well as "picking up" vocabulary in context. There is even a time and place for translation and grammar rules. The secret to successful teaching and learning probably lies not so much in the nature of a particular teaching technique as it does in the appropriate use of that technique. It is tempting to compare language learning and teaching to the preparation of a fine gourmet dinner. If a pinch of salt is called for, a half-cup can produce disaster.

One of the dangers of methodological eclecticism is that it is often aimless and uncoordinated, resulting (for the students, anyway) in a rather confusing, hit-or-miss anti-method. On the other hand, the alternatives of the past have tended to be rigidly sequenced materials or teacher-dominant classes which, although thorough and professional, are not often conducive to interaction or effective learning. Our solution to this methodological dilemma is to encourage teachers to be eclectic in a very organized and purposeful way, thus taking advantage of the strengths of eclecticism (variety) without the disadvantages (confusion and rigidity).

In a nutshell or two, the *Interplay* approach asks the teacher to think in terms of two separate-but-equal modules, a notional-functional or situation-based analytic curriculum and a grammar-based synthetic curriculum. In our view, after the beginning level, these two curricula need not and should not be locked into a rigid, integrated basal text. The teacher is encouraged to coordinate the use of the two curricula, choosing materials from each to meet the needs and interests of the students in the class.

The Interplay Approach

In recent years notional-functional and situational-based materials have become increasingly popular and available. If the students in a class are academia bound or predominantly interested in some kind of science or technology, workplace orientation, or American culture or citizenship, the teacher can find appropriate materials and then modify and use them as the basis for the analytic curriculum. Pro Lingua's interest in providing flexible functionally based materials for this purpose and our stress on communicative techniques is evident in the list of materials which follows this essay.

However, in surveying the ESL texts available, we felt that the greatest need was for grammar materials which can be used flexibly, as needed, in interplay with the students. Thus, to begin our *Interplay ESL* series, we have concentrated first on developing the grammar materials described in the introduction to this book, the two *Grammar Handbooks* and the two books of *Grammar Exercises*. With the publication of the third level in the near future, our grammar track will start with the high beginning/low intermediate level and go through advanced. For real beginners, we are planning a more integrated set of materials.

Although most of the language skills come into play in the two central curricula, we advocate supplementing them with materials of special interest. We have published several books focused on reading skills and vocabulary building. We have also brought out several "game" books. The use of games not only provides practice on specific vocabulary ad structures but establishes the sense of creative play we mentioned earlier.

Finally, we want to emphasize that when a teacher takes our *Interplay* approach of having two central modules supplemented with readers, vocabulary builders, games, and cultural activities, the basic concept of *Interplay* should be kept in mind. We don't recommend any fixed formulas such as an hour of this followed by an hour and a half of that. Once again, the appropriate use of the materials is crucial. Ideally, the teacher will be prepared with a variety of flexible materials, and the teacher and students in constant interaction will determine whether the next day, the next class, or even the next fifteen minutes should be spent on reading, writing, or playing a vocabulary game, in discussing some topic of cultural interest, or in systematically practicing a particular grammar point the students have been having difficulty with.

In summary: *Interplay* invites language learners and teachers to *inter*act with the materials, with the language and the culture, and with each other in active, creative, and productive *play*.

INTERPLAY ESL MATERIALS

The Grammar Handbook, Part 1 ♦ The Grammar Handbook, Part 2. The books, designed for in-class use, provide a simple grammar explanation, an illustrated activity sheet, and a choice of several techniques for teaching the grammar points of the lesson. Part 1 is for "false beginners" and Part 2 for intermediate students.

Grammar Exercises, Part 1 ♦ Grammar Exercises, Part 2. These two books cover the same grammar as The Grammar Handbooks, but they are designed for out-of-class use, for homework or self-study, for use with or without the Handbooks. All the exercises are contextualized for high-interest and motivation, and the answers are provided at the back of the book.

Max in America, Book 1 ♦ Max in America, Book 2 ♦ Max in America, Teacher's Handbook ♦ Max in America, Narrative Picture Poster Cards. A basic communicative skills text for adults of all ages. Book 1 is a high-beginning text for the "false beginner." Book 2 is for low intermediates. The Teacher's Handbook provides important material not given in the texts.

VOCABUREADERS

American Holidays. Exploring the traditions, customs, and backgrounds of our national holidays.

Summer Olympic Games. Exploring the individual athletic events in international competition.

The Zodiac. Exploring human qualities and characteristics. Excellent conversation starters.

Potluck. Exploring American foods and meals.

Money. Exploring the ways we use it.

LISTENING MATERIALS

People at Work. 10 real Americans interviewed in the workplace about their jobs, their interests, and their lives. 3½ hours of taped material, vocabulary and idiom exercises, discussion topics, related readings, and out-of-class experiential projects.

Stranger in Town. A "radio play" for building listening and reading skills and cultural awareness. Student script/text and tape.

Biographical Sketches for Listening. 20 winners of the Nobel Prize are described in listening passages. Workbook includes complete transcripts, pre-listening vocabulary lists, and gapped tapescripts.

VOCABULARY MATERIALS

Lexicarry. An illustrated vocabulary builder for second languages

Lexicarry Posters. 25 wall charts to facilitate classroom discussion of the vocabulary and of cultural questions suggested by the drawings.

The Interplay Approach **Appendix**

54 Function Flashcards from Lexicarry. Easy-to-handle miniposters illustrate 57 situations requiring functional language. Working together as a class or in pairs, your students will discover hundreds of critically important expressions.

Getting A Fix on Vocabulary. Using words in the news. A vocabulary builder focused on the system of compounding and affixation in English, with exercises and words in the context of news articles.

TEACHER'S RESOURCE HANDBOOKS

Language Teaching Techniques. 35 basic in-class techniques with variations.

Experiential Language Teaching Techniques. 30 out-of-class activities for learning language and culture.

Cultural Awareness Teaching Techniques. 20 discussion techniques for language classes and other training and orientation programs.

Technology Assisted Teaching Techniques. 40 student-centered techniques using 14 of the most common types of equipment from brown paper and slide projectors to PC's and VCR's.

The ESL Miscellany. A cultural and linguistic inventory of American English.

Taking Students Abroad. A complete guide for teachers.

From the Experiment in International Living — **The NEWCOMERS series:**

Opening Lines. A 1-volume, 30-lesson curriculum—4 ability levels—for ESL and literacy skills.

Shifting Gears 1 & 2. A 2-volume curriculum of 48 lessons for learning workplace skills and behavior and ESL.

Settling In 1 & 2. A 2-volume curriculum of 65 lessons for U.S. cultural orientation.

Teaching Teachers. (1) an overview of teacher training and the supervisor's role; (2) procedures and opinions on communication and feedback, training and administration, and observation and evaluation; (3) case studies of cross-cultural critical incidents; (4) plans for 20 teacher training sessions.

SUPPLEMENTARY MATERIALS HANDBOOKS

Index Card Games for ESL ♦ Index Card Games for French ♦ Index Card Games for Spanish. The 6 card games explained in each of these handbooks are easy to prepare and play using 3x5 index cards. These are student-centered, group activities which provide practice with vocabulary, structure, spelling, questioning, and conversation. Sample games are given in the target language.

Families. 10 card games for language learners. 40 colorful playing cards are included.

Conversation Inspirations for ESL. Over 1,200 conversation topics and 6 distinctive conversation activities.

For further information or to order, please write to **Pro Lingua Associates, 15 Elm St., Brattleboro, Vermont 05301,** *or call us at* **800-366-4775.**
We accept VISA and MASTERCARD orders by phone.

Appendix — Grammar and Key Word Index

a, an 115
ability 100
able to 100
abstract nouns 37
adjectives 55, 127, 130
adverbs of frequency 145
adverbs of manner 142
affirmative 1, 2, 7, 10, 22, 118
against 151
always 145
and 28
any 118
apostrophe 40
articles 112, 115
at 148, 151
auxiliary 4, 7, 10
be 4, 7, 10, 64, 67, 76
beside 151
between 151
but 28
by 151
can 100, 103
cardinal numbers 124
comma 25, 28
comparative constructions 133, 139
complement 1
compound sentences 28
conjunctions 28
contraction 22
countable nouns 37
definite article 112
demonstratives 121
descriptive adjective 127
determiner 127
direct object pronouns 46
do 7, 10, 79, 82, 91, 118
expletives 58, 61
few 139
fewer 139
for 49
frequency 145
from 154
future 85, 88
going to 85
good/bad 133, 137
have 106
have got 106
he 43
her 46, 55
hers 52
him 46
his 52, 55
how 19
I 43
imperative 91, 94
in 148, 151
indefinite article 115
indirect object pronouns 49
into 154
irregular past forms 82
irregular plural nouns 34, 37
it 43, 46, 58
its 52, 55
least 137
less 133, 139
let's 94
little 139
manner 142
many 139
mass nouns 37
may 103
me 46, 49
measurement 37
mine 52
modals of ability 100
modals of permission 103
more 133
most 137
much 139
my 55
nationality 130
near 151
negative 4, 10, 22, 79, 82, 85, 88, 91, 94, 97, 118
never 145
non-action verbs 73
non-count nouns 37
not 4, 10
numbers 124
object question words 16
of 40
on 148, 151
or 28
ordinal numbers 124
our 55
ours 52
out of 154
over 151
past tense 67, 79
permission 103
please 91, 97
plurals 31, 34, 37, 40
polite requests 97
possessive adjectives 55
possessive forms 40
possessive pronouns 52
prepositions of direction 154
prepositions of place/position 151
prepositions of time 148
present continuous 76
present progressive 76
present tense 64, 70, 76
pronouns 43, 46, 49, 52
questions 7, 10, 13, 16, 19, 25, 118
question words 7, 10, 13, 16, 19
quantity words 139
regular plural nouns 31
separable two-word verbs 109
sequence of adjectives 127
shall 97
she 43
short answers 10
simple past 79
simple present 70, 73
singular noun forms 31, 34
some 118
sometimes 145
stative 73
subject 1, 7, 10, 43
subject pronouns 43
subject question words 13
superlative constructions 137
tag questions 25
that 121
the 112
their 55
theirs 52
them 46, 49
there 61
these 121
they 43
this 121
those 121
to 49
toward 154
two-word verbs 109
under 151
us 46
usually 145
verb 1, 4, 7, 10
we 43
what 13, 16
when 19
where 19
which 13, 16
who 13
whom 16
whose 13, 16
will 88, 97
word order 1, 4, 7, 10, 13, 16, 19, 43, 76, 127
would 97
yes/no questions 7, 10
you 43, 46
your 55
yours 52

Bibliography

1. Asher, James J. *Learning Another Language through Action.* Los Gatos, CA: Sky Oaks Productions, 1982.

2. Burrows, Arthur A. *Grammar Exercises: Part One.* Brattleboro, VT: Pro Lingua Associates, 1985.

3. Celce-Murcia, Marianne; Diane Larsen-Freeman. *The Grammar Book.* Rowley, MA: Newbury House, 1983.

4. Clark, Raymond C.; Patrick Moran, Arthur Burrows. *The ESL Miscellany.* Brattleboro, VT: Pro Lingua Associates, 1981.

5. Clark, Raymond C. *Language Teaching Techniques.* Brattleboro, VT: Pro Lingua Associates, 1987.

6. Duncan, Jamie L. *Technology Assisted Teaching Techniques.* Brattleboro, VT: Pro Lingua Associates, 1987.

7. Frank, Marcella. *Modern English: A Practical Reference Guide.* Englewood Cliffs: Prentice-Hall, 1972.

8. Graham, Carolyn. *Jazz Chants.* New York: Oxford University Press, 1978.

9. Hines, Mary Elizabeth. *Skits in English As a Second Language.* New York: Regents Publishing Company, 1973.

10. *Index Card Games for ESL.* Raymond C. Clark, ed. Brattleboro, VT: The Experiment Press/Pro Lingua Associates, 1982.

11. Jerald, Michael; Raymond C. Clark. *Experiential Language Teaching Techniques.* Brattleboro, VT: Pro Lingua Associates, 1983.

12. Knowles, Phillip; Ruth Sasaki. *Storysquares: Fluency in English As a Second Language.* Cambridge, MA: Winthrop Publishing, 1980.

13. Miller, John; Raymond C. Clark. *Smalltown Daily.* Brattleboro, VT: Pro Lingua Associates, 1984.

14. Molinsky, Steven J., Bill Bliss, *Side by Side, Books 1 and 2,* Englewood Cliffs: Prentice-Hall, 1980.

15. Moran, Patrick R. *Lexicarry.* Brattleboro, VT: Pro Lingua Associates, 1990

16. Nelson, Gayle; Thomas Winters. *ESL Operations,* Rowley, MA: Newbury House, 1980.

17. Romijin, Elizabeth; Contee Seely. *Live Action English.* San Francisco, CA: Alemany Press, 1988.

18. Winn-Bell Olsen, Judy E. *Communication Starters and Other Activities for the ESL Classroom.* San Francisco: Alemany Press, 1977.